Kingdom Come

Kingdom Come

Finding Holy in the Here and Now

MELISSA ZALDIVAR

New York   Nashville

FaithWords
Hachette Book Group
1290 Avenue of the Americas, New York, NY 10104
faithwords.com
twitter.com/faithwords

First Edition: August 2019

FaithWords is a division of Hachette Book Group, Inc. The FaithWords name and logo are trademarks of Hachette Book Group, Inc.

The publisher is not responsible for websites (or their content) that are not owned by the publisher.

The Hachette Speakers Bureau provides a wide range of authors for speaking events. To find out more, go to www.hachettespeakersbureau.com or call (866) 376-6591.

Library of Congress Cataloging-in-Publication Data has been applied for.

ISBNs: 978-1-5460-1083-8 (hardcover), 978-1-5460-1081-4 (ebook)

Printed in the United States of America

LSC-C

10 9 8 7 6 5 4 3 2 1

*There are three women in the last ten years
who have awakened this book in me.*

*Andee, your incredible gift of friendship shows
me the Kingdom and Presence of God.*

Cassandra, you give me so much hope.

*Morgan, you remind me that Jesus died for
these kinds of conversations.*

CONTENTS

CHAPTER ONE

Kingdom and Presence

We ache for the Kingdom and Presence of God in every crack and corner of our lives. In every detail of ordinary life, from the tenderest moments to the ones we often overlook, there's a low hum of wonder waiting to be discovered. Of course, we don't always recognize this feeling for what it is. Instead, we feel a restlessness. A longing. So we chase it by checking things off our to-do lists, driving carpool, taking vacations, and uploading photos to Instagram. We clean the kitchen counters once the kids are down, put away junk we've absentmindedly left around the apartment, put the leftovers in the fridge, and at the end of a long day, we let out a sigh when our aching backs sink into the mattress.

•••

We ache for the Kingdom and
Presence of God in every crack and
corner of our lives.

•••

This is what I'm realizing about growing up: Things feel simple and complicated all at once. The body grows tired, and the mind keeps racing. We even set aside time to refocus but we can't seem to pay attention, and before we know it, it's back to business as usual. Like starting to stretch and breathe in deeply, only to have someone poke our ribs and pull us back into ourselves. Back to the daily grind we go with heavy eyes, reluctant hearts, and no time to entertain what might be beyond the ordinary.

Christ is in these spaces, gladly, willingly, and purposefully. Which is all good and well in theory, but what does it mean to actually live in light of that? To feel His nearness in picking up the glass you forgot was in the laundry room and sensing His sovereignty over making a sandwich? To be able to see clearly when we're surrounded by a haze of ordinary and routine and familiar and "this is just how we do things"?

A man who walked the earth the same time that Jesus did coined the Latin phrase *esse quam videri*, which means "to be, rather than to seem." There is a colossal difference between the two, but more often than not, we try to pass off *seeming* as *being*.

To put it in terms that tend to resonate, I offer you this: To *seem* is to roll your eyes as you obey. To carefully rearrange the clutter on a table and take a photo, just for a post on social media about your "messy" life. To answer a text with "K." There's something underneath it that we aren't talking about, but it's easy to see that what's being put forth is not the most honest version of ourselves. *Seeming* is what happens when we start looking to our left and our right, wondering if we should change ourselves in

2

order to be something we believe we're supposed to be. It's a facade and it will fall apart. It always falls apart.

By contrast, to *be* is to hold a crying baby for as long as it takes for her to finally slow down and you start to drift off with her as she relaxes, sweaty on your chest. To send a text telling a friend that you need someone to fight on your behalf by praying with you and for you about a big decision. To walk into a counseling office because this world is weighty and sometimes we need someone to help us lighten the load. *Being* has a lot to do with experiencing things as they truly are, finding yourself fully present and aware and honest through the good, bad, and ugly.

We know exactly what it looks like when somebody is good at *being* as opposed to *seeming*. People tend to refer to this quality by calling someone "authentic." It's a good word, but one that has been overused and is starting to lose its meaning. We crave authenticity but often are unsure of how to balance being vulnerable with keeping up appearances. (Spoiler alert: You can't have both.) When we aren't sure who we are or comfortable enough to be okay with our mess, we push into *seeming*. But every once in a while, we come across someone who has found a way to get free and knows how to live into *being* in a deep way and it is compelling.

We all know those people because they have a way of living that draws us in. They make you want to *be* in a genuine way, not just *seem* like you're the real deal. It doesn't mean they can do everything effortlessly, but quite the opposite. It usually indicates that they have put a great deal of effort into growing and learning and cultivating this quality with humility. Actual humility means someone is willing to admit when they're wrong and confess when they've sinned, and when the conversation turns to repentance, they are willing to actually go first because they know that on the other side is the grace of Jesus. And they are sure of it because they've experienced it come and wash over them time and time again. This *being* cannot be feigned because they know the cost of what it took for them to get there. Hard conversations and honest moments spent in quiet places have cultivated character that lasts. And while these people are in no way perfect, they're ready to admit to their imperfections. But it isn't just being "authentic" in a way that is actually a caricature of that word.

I once heard Jess Connolly speak at an event about the messiness of normal life. I was at this event for work and usually am pretty good at doing my job and missing out on the speakers during conferences, but this time was different. I sat in the back and she started to unpack this idea that our culture tends to pendulum swing when it comes to authenticity. We either declare, "Bless this mess!" and so deeply embrace the chaos that we're fine sitting in it and never wanting to move forward. We just shrug and say, "It is what it is," and in doing so, we can become pretty complacent in our daily life and faith, perpetually stuck in apathy.

The other side, she explained, is the measuring-up mentality. It's the place that we tend to go when the phrases that come out of our mouths are things like, "So sorry things are messy—I've been meaning to get to this," or "I know I'm not where I want to be, but I have a plan," or "I'm starting a new routine tomorrow," or "I'm working on it. In a few weeks it'll be different." We say these kinds of things when we're striving to *seem* like we're on the way to a better place rather than just having grace for where we are now.

There are days when life is messy and it's okay not to exhaust yourself trying to be some other version of yourself. And there are days when it's time to make a to-do list and tackle some projects. But when we find ourselves living from a place of constantly stressing and scheming or constantly making excuses and pretending we're above spiritual discipline, something is afoot. I'm just going to say this right now: There is grace for the overextended, but there is certainly no reason to avoid your Bible or remove yourself from a local church as a normal routine for your whole life.

There is grace for the overextended, but there is certainly no reason to avoid your Bible or remove yourself from a local church as a normal routine for your whole life.

5

I get that we have seasons where we're in a place that needs a bit of a reset, but if your manifesto is Biblical illiteracy (i.e., not opening your Bible or knowing what's in it) or *you do you* spirituality in which no one can challenge you or hold you accountable, you're doing yourself and your community a disservice.

It reminds me of a conversation that I once had with my first boss out of seminary. Her name was Jennie, and she called things as she saw them. She was one of those people who is good at *being*.

I was only a few weeks into my job and had misunderstood how something was supposed to be formatted in a document. Insecure and uncertain and really wanting to impress my bosses, I had already started to wilt under their suggestions of how my work could be improved. Looking back, it wasn't even that big of a deal, and they gave me plenty of time to take another crack at it. But there were insecurities in my own mind that told me that I hadn't just done something incorrectly but that I myself was a disappointment. Sometimes we are our own worst enemy.

Jennie sat across the table from me as I started to get teary-eyed, and something in her face changed as she leaned in a little closer.

"Melissa, I want you to ask yourself: Are you trying to measure up?"

I sat there, undone by her honest and pointed and kind question. She gently preached to me the truth that we are not called to impress people, but we're called to be confident in who it is that Christ has made us to be. That we fall short sometimes and that's okay because what matters the most isn't what we do; it's who we are. This wasn't about my competency or ability to deliver amazing work; it was about a fear deep down that I wouldn't matter, and since I based my identity on my job, I suddenly lost my value for a minute in my own mind.

This seems to be the biggest indicator of whether or not we're living the way we should: We know the difference between majors and minors—the things that matter most, and the things that matter hardly at all. And it's important to surround ourselves with those who can tell the difference between the two.

> This seems to be the biggest indicator of whether or not we're living the way we should: We know the difference between majors and minors—the things that matter most, and the things that matter hardly at all.

It has taken a few years to value, and I imagine it'll take a lifetime to build more of, the kinds of friendships that cultivate in me a sense of what matters and what doesn't. To find those people who believe God's Word and lean in and preach the truth and don't back away when things start to fall apart. Because here's what's up: The things that matter don't fall apart very easily.

I've learned to develop friendships that are deep wells rather than shallow ponds. These friends bring over vases of flowers in old sauce jars and send postcards across town with beautiful quotes written on them. They let me show up and sit down and share cold pizza that their kids left behind hours earlier. Perhaps there is no greater answer to our need for authenticity than leftover Tombstone pizza. These dear friends teach me how to be, rather than how to seem. *Seeming* makes no apologies when things get messy; *being* doesn't care about imperfection.

To *seem* demands that we pull ourselves up by our boot-straps and fabricate everything to look the way we believe it ought to look. It's why we use hashtags and take too many photos of coffee. It strips us of joy in reality and exhausts us through constant augmentation with filtering and editing. We lose sight of the fact that we were created not just to imitate, but to live out true and beautiful things by actually *existing* a different way than just copying what-ever everyone else is doing.

To *be* is far less glamorous but a precious gift to behold. It calls us to gather and check our cell phones and distractions at the door. It ventures into the risky waters of being known—actually known. And at the end of the day, it comforts us because we have allowed it to refocus our muddled sight into a clearer vision of the Kingdom and Presence of God right here, right now.

Before I go any further, I want to refresh our understanding of "Kingdom of God" and "Presence of God," so that they're at the forefront of our minds as we progress. These phrases are the foundation of the rest of this book, so I want to be clear about them now. The Kingdom of God is all that is under the rule of God our King. More than just a physical created place, but also the spiritual reality that is governed by His values and leadership and intentions. The Kingdom is both here and still coming and we see glimpses of it in relationships, work, nature, beauty, truth, and goodness.

And we know that the Presence of God is the reality of what happens when we encounter the Living God. It is His nearness—physically, spiritually, and otherwise. It has to do with understanding who God is and why it matters and how it influences who we are as those made in His image. His character and presence can be felt or unfelt but our own understanding does not and cannot change the realities of His nearness and being.

Of course, our understanding of the Kingdom and Presence of God is limited; they are far richer in reality, but I suppose that this is why this book and countless others have been written to try to explain them a bit more to our limited human understanding. We will never fully grasp them, but we have to try because the Kingdom and Presence change, influence, and define everything. When we recognize them for what they are, we realize that they are in every space, waiting to be seen and embraced.

••

Kingdom and Presence change, influence, and define everything.

••

* * *

In the Gospel of Mark, Jesus shows up and one of the first things He says is, "the kingdom of God is at hand; repent and believe in the gospel" (1:15). You've probably heard the word "repent" before, and it may carry all kinds of meanings for you both good and bad. So let's go to the root of what it means for a minute.

Simply put, to repent is to turn away from something. Imagine for a moment that you were jogging in the woods and enjoying beautiful weather (so beautiful that you were also forgetting that jogging is sometimes the *worst*). Now imagine that as you turned a corner on the trail, you saw a full-grown bear.

You would stop, dead in your tracks, and turn around. You might even jog—or run—right back home. Something in you would say, *I should not continue down this road for one more second, lest I become a cautionary tale for children.* Or you might even do that thing I do when I walk into my niece's room during naptime, silently wincing and taking careful, tiptoed steps that are right out of *How the Grinch Stole Christmas*.

Note: I know that you shouldn't run away from a bear because the bear will be more likely to chase you and win in the end, and your best bet is to slowly step away, but I'm assuming that the bear hasn't seen you because you have okay vision and saw it from a safe distance. Analogies have their breakdowns, but I think that we can all agree here that you certainly shouldn't keep cruising right up to the bear. Bears should be left alone.

Anyway—the bear. You would turn away from it, or repent. So when Jesus says, "Repent," he's talking about making a hard stop, reassessing the situation, and redirecting your route. "Repent, for the kingdom of heaven is at hand."

We repent of our sin. Sin is defined as moments we miss the mark. The ways that we treated others poorly or the way we coveted another's blessing. Things that are contrary to the character of God. A prayer of repentance in *The Book of Common Prayer* calls us to confess our sins in "thought, word, and deed, by what we have done and what we have left undone." To repent is to leave no stone unturned and to fully commit to changing our trend. To repent is to say, "Wait a second. This thing that I'm doing doesn't line up with who God is and what He does, and I'm going to turn away and ask God to realign me with the right trajectory."

∙∙

> To repent is to leave no stone unturned and to fully commit to changing our trend.

∙∙

The reason Jesus calls us to repent is a really big deal here: For the Kingdom of Heaven is at hand. Now, something we have to understand is that the Kingdom of Heaven has a whole lot to do with the way we see the world around us. Once our lens shifts to who is in charge, how things work, and what the end goals are, we will walk out our days differently. If God says that He's a sovereign King, and we are part of the great, big beautiful world He's created and rules, then we find ourselves, simply put, in His Kingdom.

Sometimes the Bible seems like it's full of foreign concepts that have very little application to us today, but nothing could be further from the truth. We understand the concept of the Kingdom, if we really think about it. The world is full of kingdoms—things like countries, provinces, and republics are all systems that, like kingdoms, organize people. You could even say that your workplace or online following is a kingdom. When you fly the flag of the Chicago Cubs or the Nashville Soccer Club, you're representing that kingdom. Likewise, when we talk about the Kingdom of Heaven, we're talking about a way or system of being, but one that is influenced by a set of values, scruples, and rules that line up with who God is and what He does.

By God's values, scruples, and rules, I want to be clear, I don't just mean morality rules. When we see God only as a rule-giver, we fail to see Him as He truly is. In the same way that parents give rules and boundaries, there are reasons for what God puts in place and it is out of a care for us and His perfection that these things are ordered. His perfection is contrasted against our humanity, in fact. When we start to think that all He wants is our perfection, we venture from *being* into *seeming* territory and our relationship with God gets out of focus.

> When we see God only as a rule-giver, we fail to see Him as He truly is.

To *seem* relies entirely on our own doing and it wears us out. *Seeming* depends on us projecting a mere image of our values to the world around us. Also, because it's not true down to our core and is only a facade, it forces us to forsake living in our true identity in Christ and is based only on what we do. It seems like a really good idea and a quick fix for social situations, but it's also inauthentic and exhausting because we're trying to control every- thing about how we are perceived, and we actually can't control anything. It will never work out. We will always be left limited by our own humanity, drained of energy from trying too hard to do the impossible. Control is an illusion and really has to do with us not trusting

God, but learning to lean into His rule is the best-case scenario.

The promise of the Kingdom is that we aren't in charge, but the One who is has our best interests in mind. We are ruled by a King who can be trusted and will direct our steps with kindness and honesty and care. We are reminded in 1 Peter 5:7 to cast "all your anxieties on him, because he *cares for you.*"

The way of the Kingdom of God is not only out of our hands but also entirely secure. Nothing shakes it. Nothing ruins or rusts or decays a single part of it. We can't earn our place within it, and our imperfections and shortcomings don't exclude us. Come literal hell or high water, it's not going anywhere. For generations, it has remained unmoved as the landscape of politics and empires has changed constantly. People have, for thousands of years, looked to the Kingdom of God as a model for the way things may not seem, but truly are.

••

The way of the Kingdom of God is not only out of our hands but also entirely secure.

••

While this may be a little scary or overwhelming or even crazy, it is also true in the best ways. When we face heartbreak, confusion, or rejection, the Kingdom of God stands firm. It is the truest foundation and the steadiest hand when we feel cracked and shaky.

And when we sit there in our doing and striving and aching for *being*—while putting our efforts into *seeming*—Jesus stands up and says to anyone who will listen, "Repent. Stop, turn around, and try *this* instead."

* * *

The second key to living in a state of being, rather than seeming, is the Presence of God. One of the reasons we really don't look through a lens of faith in all things is that we often forget that Christ is ever-present. We as Christians are reminded that we are united to Christ in a very real and intimate way. In fact, the phrase "in Christ" occurs over 160 times just in Paul's letters. His desire to be with us and His actual nearness are constant and unrelenting. While some rulers crave separation and exclusivity, our God-king desires closeness.

We often speak with great confidence about how Christ is in us, holds all things together, and is our "ever-present help," and so on. But in practice? If we are being honest, is Christ present only in that favorite Bible verse and a particularly moving chorus at church on Sunday, or does He trickle into our minds and hearts at the grocery store or a red light when we're running a few minutes late for a study group?

My first year of college, a man named Steve Saint came to speak one week for chapel. His father, Nate Saint, was famously martyred in the Amazon jungle by a tribe of people he had come to help. He was with a team of other missionaries when their plane landed in this remote place. The people of the tribe went on the defensive and, unable to clearly communicate, attacked the men, killing them.

Back at the base, their wives and children waited in deafening silence until they received the news that their husbands and fathers were dead. Steve grew up without his father and told us the story of trials he later faced, including the loss of his college-age daughter, who had a deadly brain hemorrhage in his arms.

This man who had lost so much preached to us over and over again that God is still good, even in the darkest moments. Psalm 73 reminds us that "the nearness of God is my good."

People find Christ all the time in jail cells and theaters, and in dining rooms and around campfires. But even though I believe He can be found in any place, I don't always live that way. I enter into unknown things with fear and angst rather than with the profound knowledge that He is going before me and behind me and He walks with me into those places. We don't talk in Presence language (like we don't really talk in Kingdom language), but we ache for companionship, relationship, and the assurance that we are not alone.

This is what I am learning: Everything in this life boils down to Kingdom and Presence. Every pain, struggle, and insecurity points to our need for both. Every joy, and every moment of beauty and of new life, points to the existence of both.

Not in Kingdom or Presence words, but the way this particular issue is often presented is like this: Adulting is hard. This is what we say when we lose a job, or a relationship, or our savings, or get in a car accident, or have to pay our medical bills. And more than "adulting" being hard, being a human person is hard. So let's call it what it is, shall we?

When we say that "adulting is hard," we're really just confessing that we don't have it all together and we don't know what we're doing and we're scared that someone isn't coming back for us and we are alone. We are afraid that no one is really in charge and we are doomed to fend for ourselves for the rest of our lives.

> We are afraid that no one is really in
> charge and we are doomed to fend
> for ourselves for the rest of our lives.

Let me say that if these kinds of things freak you out: Join the club. These fears are totally real, and the sinking in your stomach every time you use your debit card is shared by a lot of us.

Note: This is why Target does so well—it knows us. That dollar section carries so many random trinkets that we actually believe we're going to be able to live cutely on a budget. Their products aren't *Anthropologie*—Target is like the cousin who lives in the suburbs while big-city Anthropologie pays too much for everything. The other day someone told me a candle at Target was great because "it smells like the one at Anthro." That's why we love Target—it's a solid B-minus. And if we're real, by the end of school, a solid B-minus was more than respectable to us. Target is made for people like us because it says, "I know you want to be classy, but it's not really an option, so here's the cheaper alternative. Close your eyes and pretend this is the candle you can't afford."

We're just trying to prove that we can *adult*. But when we get home and light the Anthropologie-ish candle and feel like no one can tell the difference, we still go to bed feeling that we're inadequate because we may never afford the real thing. We wonder if we'll always live a life of trying to pass for legitimate.

And suddenly, as I write this, I see Jennie in my mind's eye as she leans in and asks a second time, "Are you trying to measure up?" I see myself at twenty-six trying to fake it 'til I make it and hoping that if I play my cards right, people will value me. In fact, much of our lives, we feel a yearning to discover a bigger world around us, and we'd love to just have a compass that could point us in the right direction. The good news is that we are craving things that already exist.

Growing up is a tricky business, and when you decide to grow up into the wrong things, those things will not deliver what you need. You'll wonder why you keep obsessing over everyone else's opinions and start to lose your sense of wonder. Pursuing the wrong things, you'll step farther and farther away from the Truth. We've all been in that place where we're in a swimming pool and go to touch the bottom and it's not there. That's what growing up into the wrong Kingdom or pushing away from the Presence of God can feel like. We become adults who don't have a firm footing anymore, and we're left to fend for ourselves—lost and uncertain.

So, it's a good thing that He comes after us, isn't it? It's a good thing He calls us by name and has known us since before we were born (see Psalm 139), and that He gives us ample opportunities to return to Him. What God desires is for us to know what's True and that starts by Him exposing what isn't true in our lives.

· ·

What God desires is for us to know what's True and that starts by Him exposing what isn't true in our lives.

· ·

Good questions can be asked over and over again in a myriad of situations and always result in exposing us in raw but necessary ways. They always get us to come clean, and help us admit that we're aligning with the wrong

19

Kingdom and trying to distance ourselves from who God is and what He does.

If you're here for every answer, I have to admit right now that I don't have them all. If you're here to read a self-help book on how to get yourself where you want to go, I'm useless to you. If you want a five-step process for "fixing yourself" and being "fine," let me tell you this: That's not the point.

On his deathbed, my grandfather looked out the window at the sunset as I sat on the floor of the hospital ready to catch him if he wavered. He had lived a long life of adventure, having had a long and successful Navy career, and I asked him to tell me his life story. He didn't talk about deadlines or bills or bargains. He told me about his uncle, who was ten years his senior, and who had taken my grandfather under his wing. He told me about spending summers with him and how he made him want to be in the military in the first place. It was the very end of World War II and people were staying away from joining, but his experience visiting his favorite uncle created a friendship and bond that made my grandfather sign up to be a pilot as a teenager. Those conversations and meals and relationships were what he wanted me to know about. At the end of his life, he didn't seem to care about adulting at all. Funny how that works.

My hope and prayer for you is that you will know deep in your bones what matters and what doesn't matter. That you will, when faced with a crossroads, choose the path that leads to the Holy Horizon. That you will be able to see clearly the invisible things and find identity and peace and great purpose in the person of Jesus Christ. And that you would clearly sense how the Kingdom of God and the Presence of God are the truest realities, giving us new life and connecting the dots between here and eternity.

You, who are weary of faking it 'til you make it: Learn to *be*, rather than to *seem*.

Turn around, and try this instead.

CHAPTER TWO

The Goodness of Nearness

The Presence of God is a peculiar thing. We yearn for His closeness, yet we hide from it like Adam and Eve in the garden. Our brokenness causes us to lose focus so we back away slowly, keeping an eye on the exit. Like learning to fall in love with someone for the first time, with God we are vulnerable and have to trust while being absolutely terrified that He won't come through. We act as though He is an inconsistent and cold deity, never truly able to reciprocate any affection that we may bring to Him.

What is it that makes us shrink away from the only thing that causes us to grow? What lies have been told that lead us to believe that God's Presence is anything less than the absolute best-case scenario? We have replaced wonder with wasteland, moving farther and farther into the desert, away from the Spring that gives us Living Water.

I think it's important right from the start to push into this awkwardness and pain. We must acknowledge the tensions we feel. Because the reality is, if you're reading this book and you're nodding along, the worst thing I can do is hand you a bunch of trite sayings and not address the root of this issue: our desire to be seen. We feel this desire almost daily, if not hourly. We want to be seen and known and experience nearness. We want people to look at us and embrace us for every good, bad, and ugly part. We want to be comfortable being present in our own skin.

This doesn't mean we want to be the center of attention. We don't all ache to be the life of the party. In fact, if you're introverted like I am, that can be a little nightmarish. No, what I mean by *being seen* is that we long to not have to explain ourselves. We want to walk into a room and be at ease. We want to be able to feel like we can unwind and not be at attention at the end of a long day. Nothing to prove, no one to impress, fully ourselves, and fully safe.

Yes, the first step to being present with God is knowing that He is truly good and trustworthy. Of course, the problem is that we're sort of hardwired from life experience to be suspicious. When someone is nice to us, it might be to take advantage. When a friend from long ago reaches out on Facebook, we wonder if they might be trying to sell us something. We can tell the difference between nice and kind pretty simply. Living in the South, I find that nearly everyone is nice, but at the same time, they might not be kind. Kindness has to do with character and motives, and niceness has to do with the way you say things. We all know someone who has wounded us while smiling or hurt us behind our backs in the name of "bless her heart." Being polite is important, but being genuinely kind is gold.

Nice is, well, nice. But kind? That's the good stuff. And

we can trust in God and His kindness. It will also aid our understanding of the Presence of God better because His kindness is one of the defining qualities that makes Him so good. He isn't smiling to our faces and talking rudely about us when we leave the room. No, He makes eye contact and cares about the answer when He asks, "How are you?"

Our God is kind. Over and over again, we see how He pursues His people when they rebel. He frees His people from slavery. He provides food for them, even though He knows that they're going to try to worship other gods. He parts the Red Sea so that they can get away from their captors. He orchestrates escapes, havens, homes, kingdoms, and triumphs so that they might know His kindness.

The Bible is written in a few languages, but the Old Testament text is written primarily in Hebrew, and it is probably my favorite language because of the richness of the vocabulary. It has this way of turning the recitation of a play into the singing of a song. And over the years as I've gotten to know the Bible in its original language, one of my favorite words is *chesed*. It's pronounced *cheh-said*, where the "ch" makes that back-of-the-throat, gravelly sound that Hebrew is known for.

Chesed is a word that is often translated as "lovingkindness," which is a powerhouse word. It's one that we don't use in everyday language, so it's faded a little bit from our English-speaking, twenty-first-century vocabulary. I can't remember the last time I said, "Man, I just feel so much lovingkindness for my nieces," or "Y'all. Lovingkindness vibes are so strong right now in my small group." But I love the Scripture of Psalm 36:7, which says, "How precious is Your lovingkindness, O God! And the children of men take refuge in the shadow of Your wings" (NASB), because this describes a God we can trust.

Lovingkindness is deep, intentional, unrelenting, and covenantal—or of the closest commitment to someone that can be made. It's more than a promise to unload the dishwasher. God's Love is a *'til death do us part* vow that cannot be broken. And isn't that just like Jesus to be described as *covenantal*? For His commitment to us to be a *'til death do us part* kind? And even more, Jesus conquered death—so there is no parting in this kind of Love.

Chesed doesn't fail. It doesn't end. It is love in its perfect form, and it is holy, bright, and overwhelming in a way we want to be overwhelmed. Over and over again, God's Love is described as lovingkindness. He Himself is this Love. He has defined it because He *is* it. Because He is kind, He wants to share that love with His people. And who wouldn't want to be seen by a God like that?

* * *

God's Presence is the assurance of goodness in the Old Testament. With our God, nothing is impossible. He appears over and over again in moments of need to remind His people that He is near to them. He is in the burning bush, warm and welcoming and holy. He is in the pillar of smoke by day and the pillar of fire by night, leading His no-longer-slaves into the Promised Land. His Presence is made known and battles are won. People are healed. Giants fall. Shepherds become kings. The barren give birth. And just when you think you've seen enough of the beauty of what happens when God comes close?

A woman finds herself surrounded by livestock and a nervous fiancé, and through blood and sweat and cries, her pain is met with joy as she gives birth to her Maker. Jesus arrives with quiet strength, a King in a manger. A helpless child who relies on his parents for survival will be their salvation. The Word of God becomes flesh and He is called Emmanuel—God with us.

Of course, He doesn't stop there. He grows up into an adult, and when the disciples want to send people away, He says, "No. Let them come." He extends His hands and heals the broken. He opens His arms and welcomes children, blessing them. He embraces those who were considered outcasts. Even in Luke 8, the woman who had been bleeding for twelve years knows that if she can just get close, everything could change.

Nearness seems to be the language of our God. Closeness and intimacy are what He desires, not just because they are nice but because they are necessary. We can't get to know anyone at a distance, and God's love language is communion.

Nearness seems to be the language
of our God. Closeness and intimacy
are what He desires, not just because
they are nice but because they are
necessary.

A few weeks ago, we gathered together in the home of someone from my church, and our pastor led us through a time of focusing on one passage of Scripture. The aim was to read it a few times and really let it sink in. I often find that when reading a passage of Scripture too quickly, part of my brain stops engaging. Perhaps it's too many years of school, where I could read so quickly but I'd find that I had read two to three pages and had not absorbed any of it. Either way, we sat in a warm living room on a rainy night during Lent and quietly listened as he read Matthew 19:13–15:

"Then children were brought to him that he might lay his hands on them and pray. The disciples rebuked the people, but Jesus said, 'Let the little children come to me and do not hinder them, for to such belongs the kingdom of heaven.' And he laid his hands on them and went away."

It was quiet. I tried to focus on the story and suddenly, I zeroed in on that phrase: *Let them come.*

Let the little children come to me and do not hinder them.

The children certainly must feel unwanted and insecure, because when they were brought to Jesus, the disciples loudly and obviously wanted to push them away. I imagined what closeness feels like now and what came to mind was a dance. A moment when I am pulled in a little closer and we move slowly, back and forth, making eye contact. There is safety and there is slowness and I am embraced.

And what I thought next, as my pulse slowed and I considered and felt the nearness of God, was, *Man. I wish that it was like this **all the time***.

Y'all, here's the thing: I think that Jesus wants us to be close *all the time.* I think He wants us to be like unhindered children or a dance partner who moves in a little more. And I know that He wants to be with us because this is the narrative of the whole of Scripture.

Paul, standing before a council of nonbelievers, says it this way in Acts 17:24–28:

The God who made the world and everything in it, being Lord of heaven and earth, does not live in temples made by man, nor is he served by human hands, as though he needed anything, since he himself gives to all mankind life and breath and everything. And he made from one man every nation of mankind to live on all the face of the earth, having determined allotted periods and the boundaries of their dwelling place, that they should seek

God, and perhaps feel their way *toward him and find
him. Yet he is actually not far from each one of us, for*
   "In him we live and move and have our being";
   as even some of your own poets have said,
   "For we are indeed his offspring."

The God of the universe does not need us, but He wants
us. He has arranged everything *so that we might feel our way
toward Him and find Him.*

· ·

The God of the universe does not
need us, but He wants us. He has
arranged everything *so that we might
feel our way toward Him and find Him.*

· ·

You know what kind of person has to feel their way toward
something? Someone who can't see. And this is a theme in
Scripture: The man born blind who is given sight by Jesus.
The way that Saul is blinded when Jesus names him Paul.
The fact that the first words spoken were "Let there be
light."

A number of times in the Old Testament, the Israelites
are reprimanded as having eyes but not seeing. And God is
not deterred by our blindness. He totally understands our
condition and the fact that as fallen people we are helpless,
unable to see the way without His illumination. So what
does He do? He arranges everything so that we might feel

our way toward Him—and find Him. He knows that we're in the dark—both literally and spiritually. But man, if He doesn't ache for us to feel our way in His direction.

I shared this insight—the one where Jesus is close and I long for it to always be that way—with my counselor the next week. We sat there in her office facing each other in comfortable white chairs and talked about presence. About how important it is to make eye contact and hear someone's voice. About how when we are separated from those we love, we are unsettled. And how Jesus doesn't want me to bring my A-game as much as He simply wants me to bring myself. To draw close.

> Jesus doesn't want me to bring my A-game as much as He simply wants me to bring myself. To draw close.

When I haven't seen someone for a long time and we're finally reunited, I'm often overcome with excitement. As we walk toward each other, I'll throw out my arms and joyfully exclaim, "Get over here!"

As I sat with my counselor, I wondered out loud how I could have missed this simple and powerful truth that God just wants to be with us. Finally, I looked at her and said, "You know, I think that three words that describe the heart of Jesus are, 'Get over here.'" My counselor started to tear up as she quietly said, "I think so, too."

So let's go back to the whole "Why we don't draw close" bit for a moment, shall we? We know that He's what we need. We know that His desire is to be with His people. We know that His nearness is our good. So what is it in us that makes us wallflowers?

Honestly, we all have different reasons. Mine has something to do with wanting to be enough and wanting to prove that I'm competent. I use a lot of "God is teaching me this lesson" kind of language because, if He's a teacher, I can keep Him at a distance of formality *and* earn His approval without it feeling too personal.

Win-win, *amirite*?

Wrong. Iamwrong.

Because that's not what He's after. Hear this: God is not trying to teach us a bunch of lessons so that we can get an A and go to heaven. He's not some celestial principal who just wants us to get into Yale. He doesn't have a book of lessons we have to be taught in order to be enough. No, God doesn't see us that way at all.

Now, let's talk about a little thing that I (and a bunch of living and dead theologians) like to call imputation. "Imputation" is a word that has to do with crediting something to one's account. If I tried to buy hair mousse (because #curlyhairhastocare), but I didn't have my wallet with me, and I was at a neighborhood salon where they knew me well, I could ask that it be credited to me. That it would be charged to my account and then paid for by me. But what if I was with my friend and she had an account and said, "No, no. Credit that to my account." Now she is the one paying for it, but I'm the one who gets the mousse. Following me? Great—because we're about to talk *theology*.

Sin has cursed everything. Nothing is untouched. All of the things are broken. Our relationships, our jobs, our hobbies, our decisions. All of them. And guess what sin does? It separates us from God. Why? Because God is holy. "Holy" is another word for "set apart." It means that He's not like us, and because He is perfectly holy and pure and good and loving and spotless, He can't be around the mess. Imagine that you are in your wedding dress when a friend runs up to you, covered in mud. You might not be able to hug her right at that moment because she's gotta get cleaned up.

Enter Jesus. Jesus is fully God and fully man. This is called the hypostatic union and it means he's not 50-50, but actually 100% man and 100% God. Hard to top. And hard to understand for sure, so don't worry if that feels like a challenge to wrap your mind around. But what you need to know is this: In order for Jesus to do what He does, He has to be who He is. So as a man, He can be on our end of the chasm. And as God, He can be on the other end—the holy, pure, good, loving, spotless end.

And Jesus, our mediator and go-between, says, "I know that the penalty for sin is death. So I'm going to die and you can take all of the sin from all of mankind and charge it to my account. I'll pay for it. Mankind gets to be holy and united to God in closeness, and I'll foot the bill to make that happen."

This is *imputation*. And it's the most powerful thing because we can never earn it back. We can never do it ourselves because we miss the mark. (See Genesis 3:1–20, where sin enters the world, and everything goes totally bonkers because we're all broken.)

So when the owner of the salon sees me walking out the door with the mousse (I know that this is a ridiculous analogy; I'm writing this late at night, I'm only twenty-eight years old, and this is my first book, so just bear with me, okay?), they don't call the police and accuse me of shoplifting. That mousse? It's entirely mine. I didn't pay for it, but I get to keep it.

Just like imputation: Jesus' blood has covered the cost, so when God looks at us, He doesn't see our brokenness, our sin, or our gross mess. He doesn't ask us to pay up or prove our worth or try to earn His love. No, He sees what Jesus has done for us in our place and we get to be close to God as a result. He looks at us and says, "Get over here." What grace.

So to review: We don't like to come to Jesus because we're afraid He'll see the mess. But He knows all about the mess because He's omniscient (He knows everything), and also when He looks at us, He sees Jesus on our behalf. And Jesus is the best-case scenario because He's perfect and He's also human; He's holy and He also loves us. There's no longer anything to fear when it comes to getting close to God. But we're still afraid. And me logically explaining this isn't going to magically take away our fear. We're still people with a past and some baggage and a few (read: *a lot of*) insecurities.

....

> Jesus is the best-case scenario because He's perfect and He's also human; He's holy and He also loves us. There's no longer anything to fear when it comes to getting close to God.

....

I want you to know that this isn't just a switch we can flip to trust God and get close to Him. We've got entire lifetimes of experience going against us. Maybe you had a parent that didn't love you well or a boyfriend that left you when you needed him most. Maybe you had a mentor who let you down or a best friend who stabbed you in the back (hopefully metaphorically, but I don't know your life). No human relationship is perfect, and all of them involve hurt.

Sara Groves said it well when she wrote a song about arguing with her husband, called "It's Me": *We hold all the keys to our undoing.*

* * *

On this side of eternity, we will face brokenness constantly. And the challenge is not letting our relationships with the humans in our lives inform our relationship with the Creator. Easier said than done. There is a tendency that we have to base our assumptions about people on our other experiences with people. The problem we face is that God is not like us. He is holy—which means He is other. And therefore, when we say, "I was hurt by a father figure so God must be a bad father as well," it often is not a fair comparison because He is so beyond our comprehension. It's a tricky place to be, considering the fact that we treat almost every other relationship this way. It's okay to be a little skeptical about God being perfect. But no matter how hurt you may be, Christ welcomes you. And He died on your behalf so that you might walk in newness of life because, at the end of the day, He desires to be near you.

Receive that.

* * *

And to be fully able to receive it, to experience nearness with the Presence of God, I think we must first address our difficulty being present with those around us. We sit down for lunch and leave our phones face up on the table. They glow and pull us away from the person we're with. And we apologize, answering the text that likely isn't urgent. Our phones give us the sense of connection, but a lot of the time, they are severing actual face-to-face experiences.

In his book on how technology is ruining connection, *Living into Focus*, Arthur Boers suggests that every time we check our phone, we are actually saying, *Something else is more interesting to me right now than what's going on in front of me.* I read that, and I refused to believe it. I told myself that I was the exception. But no matter how I've tried to get around it, I have realized that he's right. When I open Instagram while my friend is in the bathroom for two minutes, I'm aching to be distracted from the absolute bore of waiting for *two minutes.*

So it's no wonder that being present with God feels like a herculean task. If we can't even make eye contact with those around us or stay off our devices for more than a few moments, how can we sit in the Presence of God? How can we be quiet long enough to listen?

Example: Many of us have a "quiet time" by telling God what our plans are. We ask Him for specific outcomes and read a Bible verse and call it good. We start with well enough intentions, but what kind of friend would I be if I called a friend and said, "Girl, thanks for talking to me. Thanks for being my friend. I want this new job and I want my other friend to figure out her issues. I am single, but I don't want to be, so maybe I could have a husband? Also, I'm feeling stressed about my finances so could you line up some work for me? Also, thanks for talking to me. See ya!"

That would be the worst, right? No one wants, or wants to be, that friend. So why do we have these rapid-fire prayers with God? My guess is that we've turned Him into a cosmic waiter who stands there as we request what we want. Fill Him in on our plan and then say to everyone else, "I talked to God about this." We want credit for investing in a relationship without actually pausing.

Without eye contact. Without asking Him what He'd like to do. Without being present.

When we live with the mind-set that Jesus is here just to give us things, we lose sight of the fact that He Himself *is the gift.* We start to focus inward. We start to believe the lie that if Jesus is here to give us what we want as a way of showing us He loves us, then when we *don't* get what we want, or we can't "feel Him," His affection for us must have vacated the premises.

....

When we live with the mind-set that
Jesus is here just to give us things,
we lose sight of the fact that He
Himself *is the gift.*

....

If His Presence isn't enough, He's not enough.

When I think of being present in a time when it's easy to be distracted, I am reminded of a moment with my counselor back in Texas. It took a long while for me to feel present in a counseling session. I'd like to say I just did the dang thing and turned off my phone like no biggie, but it wasn't until I'd been in counseling for a few sessions that my counselor said to me, "Let me show you how to turn off notifications when you get a text."

My phone had been facedown and on silent, which *seemed* like a win, but I still left vibrate on. We'd be talking about what was going on at work or home and suddenly we'd be interrupted with the *vvv* of my cell phone. It was never an actual emergency (unless you count someone moving next week's meeting from 3:00 p.m. to 3:15 p.m. an emergency—in which case you really need to reevaluate your priorities).

But if I'm being really honest? It made me feel like I was an important person who was needed, so I let it vibrate. I let it interrupt as if to say, "This person sitting here working through her junk is actually very important and you should be so lucky as to have a moment of her time." I let it nag me occasionally, and when I appeared to ignore it, I felt like a hero. As if it were the honor of a lifetime for this counselor to have my attention.

Look at me not looking at my phone. I am so disciplined and we are so blessed. In some way, I just wanted to matter. To seem important. To be needed in multiple places at once. What irony—Christ actually *is* those things, so I put Him on the outskirts and avoid eye contact.

When my counselor asked me to silence—truly silence—my phone, she knew, as did I, that I was an adult, fully capable of doing such a thing. But what she was actually doing was inviting me to practice what I was preaching. The truth is that we distract ourselves constantly, because we're afraid that if we don't post the right photos or caption with the right words, we're going to be found out. If we don't keep moving from image to image, we'll be forced to reconcile with the fact that our life isn't social-media perfect all the time. Comparison steals our peace, and inadequacy threatens to destroy our well-built facades.

Sometimes I don't want Jesus all up in everything because I want Him to perceive me as more perfect than I actually am. I want to be this pious person with something to offer Him. I want to be able to come to Him and tell Him what's new and I want Him to say, "Wow. That's super interesting and I'm not looking at my phone right now because I am impressed."

We crave acceptance.

We ache for belonging.

We desire nearness.

We long for closeness.

And those are the right things to want. We were wired to want them, in fact. But when we search for those things in the wrong places? When we search for acceptance on social media or in relationships that will inevitably let us down? When we refuse to make eye contact with our Savior because we're looking for fulfillment elsewhere? We miss out.

So how do we start to understand the Presence of God? One day at a time, my friend. In the same way that you typically don't get married on a first date, you have to start small to become near with God. Take a step forward. Turn off your phone. Open the Word of God and see for yourself why His Presence is a big deal. Pay attention to how Jesus responds to people. Notice the ways that God calls His people to Himself. See the bigger narrative of the Presence of God and start to understand that He is moving all things so that you might feel your way toward Him. Keep in mind that in His unrelenting *chesed*—lovingkindness—He wants you close.

Oh, that you might hear His voice, beckoning you like a child. Calling out, "Get over here."

CHAPTER THREE

Kingdoms and Kings

A few months ago, I crossed the ocean to Great Britain for the first time, and it was one of those trips that was exactly what I imagined it would be. I found myself in St. Andrews, Scotland, walking down old streets of this town that has rested for centuries on the edge of the North Sea. It was cold, but not too cold, and plenty wet. My friends David and Anna had gone over for David's Ph.D. a few years earlier, and I always said I wanted to come visit them before he finished his program. Then my friend Chesney got married to a man named Preston and he became a student at St. Andrews, too. I took it as a sign that I simply had to take a few days and venture to this city before they all moved back stateside.

The city itself was quaint and charming, and I could have easily imagined myself staying forever in that kind of place. It was the sort of town that at the same time made you want to take both a long walk and a long nap. Cafés and grocery stores bordered the university and its many buildings strewn throughout town. Just around the corner from David and Anna's apartment, right on the edge of a cliff, was the St. Andrews Castle, built around

1200 AD. Now in ruins, it still stands tall, a haunting reminder of the power of kingdoms. In its heyday, it must have been a majestic sight, made of dense layers of stone, housing important events in church history. There's a part of my brain that is absolutely curious about the idea of a kingdom. Living in a democracy makes it challenging to understand the implications of statements like "The Kingdom of God is at hand." We imagine it as a sort of country that exists somewhere out there, but not as a place that could be felt around the globe. Our upbringing makes us think of terms like "senator" and "state" and "federal" and "president." We consider the borders of a country, and there are hundreds of other countries much like our own, full of people and laws and rulers. We have countless cultures in a myriad of government systems. And kingdoms also have a way of feeling downright magical.

This might be the reason that a group of girls from my dorm and I woke up at 4:00 a.m. on April 29, 2011. Every detail had been obsessed over—the uniform that Prince William wore and the dress designed for Kate Middleton. We all gathered, in shirts we had made for our royal wedding–watching, around the TV on the first floor of our dorm building. With snacks in hand, we cheered and offered commentary in badly imitated British accents. There was something about the story of royalty that transfixed us. It's the reason we start stories for children with phrases like, "Once upon a time in a kingdom far away, there lived a princess…" and not, "Once upon a time, in a nation far away, there was a president's daughter…"

Yes, a kingdom feels magical and foreign to us. But we forget the reality that here and now we find ourselves deeply within the boundaries of the Kingdom of God and never take time to consider it. So in the name of starting this story where we must—at the very beginning—let's venture back to Genesis 1.

See, God didn't haphazardly or randomly create the world around us. Rather, He was systematic and intentional in how He did it. He created a network of kingdoms (that is, places) and kings (that is, inhabitants) that would be built and filled. He did so in a way where there was order and clarity and a structure. And now we look back to that structure to remember how things were originally created and what His good plan was in making all of it.

Typically, Genesis 1 starts like this in my head: "In the beginning, God created the heavens and the earth and the earth was formless and void and the Spirit was hovering over the waters" (vv. 1–2). It seems a little strange and precious and maybe even confusing. The scene is set and it almost feels like you've stumbled into the middle of something that was already unfolding, mid-sentence. So let me give you a literal translation from the Hebrew, to paint a clearer picture:

In the beginning, created by God, were the heavens and the earth. And the earth was formlessness and emptiness and darkness was on the face of the deep. And the Spirit of the Lord hovered tremendously on the face of the waters.

45

Suddenly, the Spirit of God isn't a little floating ghost. Rather, it's hovering with eager anticipation and awareness and power. And "hover" is in the *piel* tense, which is one of emphasis. It's what turns "broken" into "shattered," if you will. When words are in the piel tense, it's like turning the volume to 11, breaking the knob off.

If this were a movie, it'd be set in deep space to a low bass hum, and at an epic moment of total edge-of-the-seat anticipation. That word meaning to "hover tremendously" is a loaded gun. It shows up another time in Deuteronomy 32:10–11:

> *He found him in a desert land,*
> *And in the howling waste of a wilderness;*
> *He encircled him, He cared for him,*
> *He guarded him as the pupil of His eye.*
> *Like an eagle that stirs up its nest,*
> *That hovers over its young,*
> *He spread His wings and caught them.* (NASB)

Authoritative and strong and ready. *The Spirit of the Lord hovered tremendously on the face of the waters.* And that's just in the first two verses.

Something is coming. Something is about to begin. Out of the formlessness and emptiness and darkness, there is a voice—the voice of God. And He says, "Let there be light" (v. 3), and there was light. Now, this is something we need to realize up front about the power of God: when He speaks, things happen. When He uses commands, what was not there before is suddenly very much so there. He says "light," and light bursts forth.

When He merely speaks, creation literally begins—and He's just getting started. The light is separated from darkness and He names them "night and day." And He calls the light "good." Day One was good.

The water systems of sky and land are created—clouds and oceans and rivers and lakes. Ecosystems can now flourish, rivers and seas and morning dew start to form from nothingness. Day Two was good.

Separated from the water, land comes into existence—mountains and valleys and hillsides and beaches. And from it? Trees and vines and vegetables and fruits and bushes and flowers and moss start to spring forth. Day Three was good.

Next, the stars swirl out in space, shining down alongside the sun and moon, offering orbs of beauty and light that travel through the sky, marking time and seasons, influencing the tides, warming the land, and giving people a way to navigate on the high sea. Day Four was good.

God says in Genesis 1:20 , "Let the waters swarm with swarms of living creatures and let birds fly above the earth across the expanse of the heavens." Suddenly, there are all kinds of fowl and fish, making their way through the waters, climbing into the trees and soaring over canopies of forest and across vast expanses of creation. Day Five was good.

And as if things weren't exciting enough, God adds in some animals and, finally, people. Creation is full of life and vibrancy and order. He formed man out of the dirt of earth, breathing life into his lungs. (See Genesis 1:1–31.)

A while back, I was with my dear friend and her son, who was about eight years old at the time, and we were telling him and his sister the story of creation. Afterward, we asked them, "So what can we remember about this story?" Her son had seemed like he was distracted and only half paying attention, but when asked that question, he simply stated, "God took something he loved—the earth—and used it to make something he loved even more."

This is the beauty of creation: God is good and made man to take charge of it all—what a gift to entrust to us. He did all of this creation with purpose that He then handed to us because He cares for us deeply, not just because He was bored.

All of creation is ordered in what we call a system of "kingdoms and kings." He didn't just make a bunch of things He thought would be cool to make but created places, and then filled them with something that would inhabit them. He is a God of order and intentionality right from the start of everything.

I'll lay it out this way:

Day One: Heavens and Earth
Day Two: Sky and water systems
Day Three: Dry land and vegetation
Day Four: Stars, moon, and sun
Day Five: Birds and fish
Day Six: Land animals and people

Day One's creation is filled on Day Four, Day Two's creation is filled on Day Five, Day Three's creation is filled on Day Six. Everything has a place; every place has an inhabitant. God has created a perfect Kingdom that He rules over with no conflict. The relationships are perfect. Untouched by sin, this place is a paradise.

Adam, however, is alone. It's the one thing so far that God has explicitly said is *not good*. And so God puts him deep under and creates Eve in a final act of this new creation. She is stunning and mesmerizing, and an awe-struck Adam delights in her. She is created because it is not good for him to be alone and this is something we need to remember: Eve was made because God wanted man to have community. She brought more than just companionship—she would be the one who birthed new life to mankind, the mother of all the living.

Adam and Eve were unashamed and whole and in perfect relationship in the garden that God had placed them in. But there was a tree that was about to change everything. See, in the Bible, trees are often important. You're cursed if you hang from a tree and it's often a sign of judgment, but this tree—before sin entered the world—was a sign of life and power. It was off-limits and they only had one job: Take care of the earth and stay away from the tree of the knowledge of good and evil, also known as the tree of life.

In the beginning, things start with something good and abundant and perfect. And when we get that and feel the weight of the beauty and flawlessness of the world that has been made, and soak it in moment by astounding moment, we almost want to cry out to Eve as she's walking alone in the garden. As she hears the voice of a crafty serpent. We want to tell her to stop listening, to not even turn around, to never even consider it.

But she does, and so does Adam. They sin, and everything breaks.

And when it breaks, it happens in all the worst ways. The fall of mankind happens and sin ripples across the edges of the newly formed seas, moving across the plains and deserts, dipping into valleys and saturating the pristine forests. It enters the world and touches every single part of it. Suddenly, a clock has started ticking, and when it stops, death comes.

The Kingdom of God is suddenly masked by a thousand deceptions and avoidances around every corner. People now carry darkness in their hearts, motives ruined and minds manipulated. At the start of Adam and Eve's existence, God gives them two directives: Cultivate and keep.

Cultivate the land. Take good care of it and water it and grow good things and harvest in the seasons of each plant's time. Also, they were called to keep. "Keep" is a word that means to guard or protect something. Protect the land to help it thrive.

The next time that we see those two words, sin has seeped into the world. And now? We learn that, as a result of the brokenness, thorns will be cultivated from the land, choking out the plants that the man is trying to grow.

Adam and Eve leave the garden and an angel was placed at the entrance to guard it from them coming back in. The same Hebrew word for "keep" is used here. Only now, instead of them protecting creation, it is guarded from them. The layers of heartbreak in this moment are too many to even try to count.

One afternoon, I was walking in the woods behind my friend's house. It was a pristine stretch of Tennessee woodland that was brilliantly green and full of life as the spring had offered warmth and rain to cause it to bloom. I put on my rain boots and coat to walk around along the paths that wove throughout the property and I wondered for a moment, *What if this was what the first moments of creation were like?* Suddenly I was filled with a childlike joy as I wandered deeper and deeper into the trees, putting my hands in front of me, pushing back branches and stepping with more and more confidence until I was suddenly stopped dead in my tracks.

A long, thick, thorny plant had grown up and stretched itself across the path before me. It wasn't a rose or something beautiful; it was something menacing and dangerous, with thorns nearly an inch long. I traced it as it moved not only up, but across, wrapping around the nearby trees and other foliage. My joy turned to a somber and dark reality: Even the most beautiful of woods are marked by those thorns. Even in the middle of a path perhaps no other person has walked in years, there was a vine of thorns. As I looked past it,

I saw that there were more thorny vines and they were slowly taking over this strange little patch of land. I carefully stepped away, suddenly over-aware of my surroundings, and made my way back to the house. I made a cup of peppermint tea and remembered the beauty of the walk, but my mind keeps wandering back to that one moment of juxtaposition.

So now, the Kingdom seems to be divided into what was and what is. Perfection and present situations. Communion and coping. The perfect paradise is lost, and now Adam and Eve have to navigate two Kingdoms in one place—the one that reflects the glory of God and the one where sin desires try to overtake the beauty surrounding it. Like a thorn wrapping itself around a healthy vine, there is a fight between these two Kingdoms. And we know that the Kingdom of God will win out in the end, but in the meantime, there is a brokenness that has to be faced.

Things get more and more messy, with the next generation experiencing murder and things spiraling out of control from there. When we flip through the pages of the Bible, there seems to be not one person who lives a simple and easy life. Instead, it's a book full of people trying to reconcile the fact that we're living in a kingdom that is haunted by sin, trying to constantly pull itself apart. Still, we know that the Kingdom of God is here in some way because God is still sovereign over it all—

his kingliness has not changed at all. And as the story of redemption continues to unfold, we are moving toward the end when all will be made right and we will see the Kingdom as it truly is with never-ending light and life and flourishing. The Kingdom here and now sometimes seems impossible to detect, because we are surrounded by constant distraction and deception, but this is why Jesus proclaimed it as both present and coming—it's not what we see with our eyes that shows us the truest reality of the state of things.

· ·

The Kingdom here and now sometimes seems impossible to detect, because we are surrounded by constant distraction and deception, but this is why Jesus proclaimed it as both present and coming—it's not what we see with our eyes that shows us the truest reality of the state of things.

· ·

God's Kingdom is eternal and still very-much-so exists, but we don't get to experience its fullness as long as we're living in this broken world. We call this *realized eschatology* or the *Now, but not yet.* It means that while we can still look at creation and sense God and experience His Kingdom that He made for us right here, right now, we have to accept the fact that there are parts that we will one day know...but not yet.

So how do we come to understand God as a King, especially if we don't live in a monarchy that has one? Let's go back to the Book on this one.

A king can't just be anyone. There are certain qualities that must be part of a kingly identity. For example, a king is completely in charge. This means that He is sovereign—all is within his jurisdiction. A king is also strong and a ruler in charge of all the needs of his people. God is a good King who has something great in mind for us. And when we forget who He is as our King, it is easy to live in a world in which He no longer carries power. Or at least in one where we act like He carries no power.

The thing about the Kingdom of God is this: It exists whether or not you choose to believe it does. Just like God is good, even in darkness. Just like love is true even in distance. We are faced with a choice in every moment. We can choose to acknowledge the reality that the Kingdom of God is our truest home, or we can decide that the kingdom of man is all we will ever recognize. We can choose to live our lives with a wider lens of God's Kingdom, or we can turn a blind eye to it, living for ourselves and what we want to see.

....

> Just like God is good, even in
> darkness. Just like love is true even
> in distance. We are faced with a
> choice in every moment. We can
> choose to acknowledge the reality
> that the Kingdom of God is our
> truest home, or we can decide that
> the kingdom of man is all we will
> ever recognize.

....

Last summer, I bought a new car. Well, new to me. It's a 2011 Honda CR-V, and I love it. I did not name it because I'm not the kind of girl who names cars, but nevertheless, it seems to suit me well. This car is a middle-of-the-road sort of vehicle. Not the fanciest, but certainly better than what I had before.

See, I used to drive a 1998 Buick Century. It was a monster of a car that felt a lot like driving a boat. It was *solid* in the winters of New England during seminary and was one of those cars that served me well until it totally fell apart. First the power steering went, then the transmission. They told me that basically nothing else could happen to this car because it still had pretty low mileage. The only thing that might go wrong and be super expensive would be if it blew a head gasket.

Guess what blessed thing happened two months later?

You got it—head gasket. Since I'd paid so much for this car to be fixed already, and fixing it would cost about the same amount as buying another car for which I hadn't already bought a brand-new transmission, engine, and power steering system, I decided—like a genius—to pay for repairs. Truth be told, I for *sure* had to borrow money from my parents for it because I worked at a nonprofit and couldn't afford it. I'm still paying them back for it. (P.S. Thanks, Mom and Dad!)

Finally, the car bit the dust, with more problems that would be another 400 bucks to fix and I just gave up. I couldn't get behind the little Buick, so I sold it. I figured I had to have one of the last '98 Buick Centuries out there. Turns out, I was wrong.

For weeks—no, months—I saw the same car every-where. At first, I thought, *Oh! It's my car with its new owner!* but it would have some random dent or an old bumper sticker, and one day I realized that I just had '98 Buicks on the brain. Isn't this the way things go? You notice something or think about it, and suddenly, it is absolutely *everywhere.*

This is what I have found about the Kingdom of God, too. We have to retrain our eyes to see it, but once they adjust and catch a glimpse of the Kingdom, everything is clearer. Suddenly, weddings aren't just crazy, stressful dance parties. No, they are mirrors of the Kingdom of God, reminding us that God wants to have communion and union with us. And music isn't just a nice series of sounds, but it tells tales of the human condition and paints pictures in our imagination of what life is like when seen in a new light. Even our meals change because they aren't just giving us life—we're seeing that man still cultivates from the earth, even though it's really hard work. And we get to be sustained because of it, the way things were originally intended.

The nature of the Kingdom of God is still found before our very eyes; we just have to know what we're looking for.

So if God is a King and we're in His Kingdom, what does that make us? As we know, Kingdoms have all kinds of socioeconomic classes. There are caste systems that some are born into and can do nothing to escape. There is no upward mobility if you're born into the lower class of many cultures, but if you're high up on the social class chain, you might just fall out of place into poverty if you aren't careful.

Relationships in many kingdoms are highly political, which leads to corruption. We're all a bunch of sin-marked people, remember? We would like to believe that humanity as a race has moved past that kind of behavior, but the reality is that more people are enslaved today than the 1800s. People are in forced labor camps, children are exploited, woman are prostituted, and the elderly are abused. When left to our own devices, people abuse people all the time. I don't say this out of cynicism as much as realism. Because when we look at this whole narrative—Creation, Fall, Struggle, Redemption—we can see that we're not where we're supposed to be, and we're not fully healed yet.

In the Kingdom of God, however, there are different

rules that our King has put into place. Rules like the Ten Commandments, which remind us not to be envious, or steal, or kill, or disrespect, or run after the wrong things. Through the Commandments, God urges us to dignify one another, and welcome the refugee, and care for the orphan, and look after the widow. He pursues people over and over again because of His rich love, and it always results in people feeling seen, known, and cared for. This is the rule that our King has put in place. These are the ways that we ought to see each other.

So when we come to places where we are tempted to think less of someone or to shame them for something, we can see them with new eyes, recognizing that the Kingdom of God is still here among us and the kingdom of man is trying to rip us from God and one another. We start to realize that we are all marked by sin and trying our best, and in those moments, we can offer grace and forgiveness and "let's try that again" because we believe Him when he says, "I am making all things new."

I once found myself in a situation where I felt taken advantage of. I didn't want to be overly dramatic when I told my counselor the story, or admit how much I had been hurt, so whenever she asked if I felt hurt, I would push it aside and say, "It's really fine. I am sure that I was somehow in the wrong." Then one day she said what would be one of the most defining statements of my last few years: "In the Kingdom of God, people are subjects— not objects."

What she meant by that is that we are not here to prove

our worth or our legitimacy. We are not called to judge one another and try to get to a higher class in the Kingdom. We are all subjects in this Kingdom. We are all under the rule of the Most High King. And we are not to use and abuse and objectify others. When we decide that our social standing in the kingdom of the world is more important than the dignity of another person, we have made them an object. When we see them for what we want to get out of them rather than for who they are, we have made them an object. When we look at them and only think of the issues that we disagree on or the style that they wear that makes them less fashionable, or the job that they have that we consider a low-income—and therefore unimportant—job, we have made them an object.

For years, the people of Israel asked for a king because they wanted to have someone to put on a throne. God was not King enough for them because, when they looked around, the other nations had kings in charge who stood on platforms and gave great speeches. God tried to explain that He was enough, but they refused to accept this. So he gave them a king.

And every king they had? Not the best. First was King Saul, who was the real deal as far as pomp and circumstance were involved. Strong and valiant and popular. But Saul was jealous and corrupt, and when he got wind that David—a shepherd boy—was chosen by God to be the next king, Saul hated him. He was murderous toward David, and David had to flee from Saul, even though his best friend was Saul's son.

When Saul died, David became king. And he was a good king who wanted to please God. They called him "a man after God's own heart." But he was still human, and one day took a man named Uriah's wife, Bathsheba, and forced her to sleep with him. She could not say no to the king, but Scripture always refers to her as "Uriah's wife" as a way of saying, "She wasn't David's."

David repented of his sin but damage was done, and when his son, Solomon, took the throne, it felt like there could be hope because he was wise in many ways. But he still carried lust in his heart and kept women in his palace whom he objectified. After that? The Kingdom of Israel split and went into exile.

And then, when Jesus showed up on the scene, no one believed that He could be the king that Israel had been promised when God said, "I'll give you a king now, but one day you'll get the real deal."

Jesus arrives and he's not what people expect. But he comes talking about the Kingdom of God. In fact, I mentioned earlier that the first words recorded by Him in the Gospel of Mark are, "The time has come, and the Kingdom of God is at hand. Repent and believe in the gospel" (1:15). Remember that phrase? Turn around and try to live life through the lens of the Kingdom of God. Jesus spoke about things that felt in direct contrast to the kingdom of the world. He told people to love and serve and sacrifice for one another. There's no jargon in his preaching about getting ahead or finding success or being better than the people around you. No, He is looking through the lens of the Kingdom of God, and in that world, we are loved, and seen, and valuable because a good, Kingly Creator made us.

In contrast to the worldly kings of nations around him, Jesus was lowly and kind, and the crowd of bystanders watched him get nailed to the cross and mockingly put up a sign above the cross that said, "King of the Jews." They scoffed as he suffocated and bled for hours before finally dying.

Three days later, He appeared to some women, fully alive. Jesus our King? He had conquered death. And He stayed around for forty days before ascending to heaven, but before he went, he said, "Listen. I'm coming back." And we're promised that when He does, He will be exactly the king we need. And He will rule, and the Kingdom of God will be fully understood. But for now, we find ourselves in a precarious place of longing for better while living in broken. And while it's tempting to scramble and panic and just try to fix it all, we can't possibly make every piece new again. We are certainly called to practice justice and mercy (in fact, this is how we build the Kingdom), but we also have to remember that until He makes all things right, sin will keep destroying. But we can fix our eyes on what He has laid out for us; we can search for the Kingdom in our everyday lives and work hard to bring His Truth into the world around us.

So we know the history of God's people and kings, but who are we in His Kingdom? This is the really crazy part: We aren't just a bunch of lowly servants or serfs in this

Kingdom. Instead, we are called "co-heirs" with Christ. This means that all of the inheritance of the Kingdom is ours. Back in the day, when someone would die, they would leave everything to the heir, who was often the first-born son, and the son could do with that fortune whatever he wanted. But Jesus, in His kindness and gentleness and kingliness, says, "I just want you to share in this with me." And we aren't given just a piece of the Kingdom; we are given all of it.

This entire idea was unheard of in the Ancient Near Eastern context in which it was established. Heirs and in-heritances were a very big deal. And because of the mercy of God, we are called sons and daughters, adopted into relationship with God as our Father. Because of this, we now have the opportunity to inherit the goodness of the Kingdom of God. Christ's sonship was the way into this arrangement, and as we are united to Him in His death and resurrection, we are therefore included in the family of God, and that actually secures our status in the Kingdom as those who partake in this divine inheritance.

Even though we're broken. Even though we're sinful. Even though we argue with our families and get annoyed by our co-workers and yell at the people who cut us off in traffic. Even when we strive to stake a claim in the kingdom of man, we are given the Kingdom of God. Why? Because there is a King and he just wants to be with us again.

He wants communion with us, the way that he intended it back in the garden, when the whole Kingdom was created. He made rules for this Kingdom that give us value and worth and love and beauty and redemption. He knows that the world is fighting for our affection, longing to distract us from seeing the Kingdom that is around us. He's standing there, giving everything for us, sacrificing Himself so that we might inherit all of what was intended to be ours. From the very beginning, as the Spirit of God hovered tremendously in anticipation of all of this, until the moment that Jesus makes everything right again, our King has a good plan, and in Revelation 22:5, we see how it all ends with the restoration of Light and redemption for all creation:

> *And night will be no more. They will need no light of lamp or sun, for the Lord God will be their light, and they will reign forever and ever.*

This, perhaps, is the most beautiful reality of the Kingdom of God: It is here, it is coming, and we get to watch it all unfold as co-heirs to its riches.

CHAPTER FOUR

Safety Is Not Simple

A re you writing this down?"

There we sat in two overstuffed white chairs, facing each other in the sort of way that makes you feel like there's no place else to go. The sort of way that begs for you to just be present. No phone. No interruptions. Just one hour of facing another human being, talking about what is actually happening in your head and your heart.

I had just told her about the fact that I was struggling to actually be present and it was ironic, because I was about to write this here book on the Presence of God. She wasn't being mean or sarcastic when she asked if I was writing down what we'd been talking about because she knew, as well as I did: To write a book, you have to live it out. I'd hoped that every lesson to be learned had already occurred in the past, and so as I approached this book, I'd just sit down and tell you all the things I knew to be true because they were proven to me years ago.

But no. That's not how this works.

"You should be writing this down." She smiled.

My counselor is kind and it shows in her face. She was right, and I slowly put down my weapons of self-preservation and pride and let her invitation sink in. She was reminding me that if we don't write things down, we might forget them. Of course, in a counseling office, sometimes you wish you could forget. Sometimes, you're walking through some really dark, heavy stuff and the last thing you want is to remember it all.

While counseling is a good and beautiful thing, the hardest part is probably the fact that you get found out. You have counseling sessions on good days and bad days and you trust this person with the anxious, messy moments that you'd rather shove to the side. My counselor has an extra gift for seeing right through the ruse I like to put up. She slows me down, and while it's exactly what I need, it's not entirely comfortable when you're used to flitting from thing to thing to avoid seeming incompetent.

I'm sure I'm the only person who feels this way. The only one who has been afraid of the vulnerability of being painfully honest with another person. Oh, wait—we all feel this way at one moment or another.

Counseling has been this space where I force myself to lose the filter that I tend to attach around different groups of people. This honesty allows me to just cut the act and get to the root of what's really going on. As far as I'm concerned, if you're skirting around the issue in counseling, you're wasting their time and your money. No one gets well by telling the doctor half of the symptoms and leaving out the part where you can't stop coughing up blood.

Sometimes, therapy feels like a tidal wave that you watch coming toward you. I once read that it takes several seconds for someone to respond to a shocking or overwhelming sight. That sounds about right. What's coming at you is strange and unknown, and in the movie *The Day After Tomorrow*, when there's a series of tornadoes in downtown Los Angeles, a guy just stands by the window and stares. He's that character that you believe is just a total fool for not moving because HELLO A TORNADO IS COMING FOR YOU, but now I kind of get it.

I've survived a few tidal waves in the counseling office now, and as they grow on the horizon and get close, I still feel fear, but there's a little bit of bravery in there, too. Sometimes, when my counselor asks me to focus or we're about to face down something particularly scary, I physically change position a bit. I put my hands on the edge of the overstuffed chair's armrests and uncross my legs, both feet pressing firmly onto the floor. I might take off my glasses and rub my tired eyes like a two-year-old fighting off a nap. Sometimes, when I am extra worn, that action makes me start to cry.

I don't know what I thought I was getting myself into the first time I walked into a counselor's office. I was about nineteen years old, some heartbreak had happened thousands of miles away, and it had left me in a place I'd certainly been before, but one that needed support in a way that I hadn't known existed. I'd never darkened the door of one of the rooms where the chairs face each other, but

I showed up because I'd made the appointment, it's what I was supposed to do, and I'm a rule follower.

Maybe I thought it would be a short stint that was a catch-all for any kind of problem that could pop up in the future. You know the story: Go to counseling at nineteen and never deal with anxiety or stress down the road. Go to counseling and the pain of the past won't exist anymore. Go to counseling and you can be fine and on your way. I've spent a lot of my life trying to be fine.

We usually don't share our stories in the middle, when the night is long and it doesn't feel like the sun will rise. We don't share what it feels like when we're panicking and unraveling and nothing is clean and shiny and put together. We're so afraid of feeling unsafe that even the mention of our own fear feels scary. We wonder "what would people think of me if they knew how afraid I am?"

There are countless times when our grief or pain or fear has been met with a trite Christian saying or mention of "God won't give you more than you can handle." (Which is not at all true. Angie Smith says, "Everything is more than we can handle!" and she is *right*.) When true vulnerability is shared with someone unsafe, we end up feeling ashamed and small. So we stop telling people what's truly going on out of wanting to be safe again. It's easier to be quiet than to be honest. We'd rather be perceived as put together than exposed and pushed off to the side.

And then? We worry that God Himself wants us to be

put together. That when it comes to His reaction to our dark side and our baggage and our fears, it's all smiles and nods, but deep down He probably thinks we're crazy. And that maybe Jesus Himself isn't truly safe. That He's just as conditional with His love as people are. That if we step in the wrong way or say something uncouth or admit our own weakness, He will walk out the door, taking with Him His very Presence.

And what we crave is that Presence. That willingness to step forward. That nearness and intimacy and eagerness to enter into our mess and say, "Can I join you?"

This is the tension that I feel as I write this chapter: I know that Jesus is safe, but I don't treat Him that way. Even when things seem to be fine between us, there's hesitancy. Today, my counselor saw it and said, "Are you angry with Him over the grief you're feeling?"

"No," I said.

A pause. She made eye contact and waited.

"Well, maybe a little. I mean, after it happened, I was driving and felt like Jesus was so near. He was such a comfort in my mourning...but then, I remembered that He's in control of it all and it made me start to cry."

She kept waiting.

"And I guess that feeling boils down to the fact that I like to separate God into parts. When my heart is broken, I completely accept that He wants to comfort me. But at the same time? I don't want to accept that He has allowed the pain to happen in the first place. And while I think about that—" My voice stopped working as I let out a tearful laugh and tried to breathe normally. I started to cry and shake my head back and forth and just pointed to my face, unable to make words. Finally, after I rolled my watery eyes and grabbed another tissue, I looked at her and said, "Yes. I think that there's something there."

Last year, I moved into a house for the first time alone. It's a tiny two-bedroom, one-bath built in 1928. I had just gotten a new job that didn't make my parents nervous (because ministry jobs do not equal outstanding pay), and it felt like I was finally a legitimate adult. I had done hard work and saved my money and gotten a job that would allow me to buy avocados without over-thinking it, and on top of all that, I'd just signed with a literary agent a few weeks prior. In short, the world was my oyster. I had nothing to prove because I had already proven that I was responsible and finally fine.

And then, because the joke's on me, a few unexpected financial situations arose and I found myself with 7 dollars in my bank account (an amount I didn't even want to type right here in this book for people to read, but I'm trying to tell the ugly truth) with a car full of friends in another state. They were helping me move some things from my aunt's house in Alabama, and while I was there, I happened to check my bank account, and as I stared at my single-digit balance, I was in shock. So I did what anyone would do: I went outside of the place we were having lunch, sat on the curb, and started to cry.

I couldn't tell my friends I was suddenly strapped for cash and I didn't know how I would pay for gas for the trip back. In an effort to gain some control, I called my car insurance company to add renter's insurance (because that's a whole thing), thinking it was something to check off my grown-up to-do list. On that call, however, they informed me that I was past due because of a mix-up, and if I didn't pay them 134 dollars immediately, I was going to be uninsured. In a different state. With a car full of friends who were helping me out.

I explained to the nice woman that I actually didn't technically have more than 10 dollars in my bank account and she explained that it was about time I called in a few favors because *tough luck you have to pay right now because that is how the world works, it's called capitalism and didn't you learn this in high school econ class or something?*

I panicked. And I paced. And I accidentally stepped on a dead bug on the sidewalk, which just added to how gross I felt on the inside, and finally, I called my parents, who were proud of me being an independent adult, and I asked for the money. I started to cry on the phone, and through tears all I got out was, "I'm so sorry."

I was overcome by my found-out-ness in a way that I'd never known. I felt so immature and unprepared, as if all of the work and achievement and adulting I'd done had fallen apart when I thought about my bank account and the situation I was in. And I wondered: *How do we face the people around us when we come up so short?*

* * *

The Bible is full of people who loved God and also felt the weight of a broken world. And while they may have lived in a very different time and place, they were still human beings, who shared the same experiences many of us face today. Even after they initially encountered God, they still had to prepare meals and work jobs and raise kids and step outside of their comfort zones. Sometimes their circumstances got better; sometimes they got worse. There's a reason that Scripture reminds us to have gratitude "in all circumstances" (1 Thessalonians 5:18). The fact of the matter is that we will face a variety of circumstances because that's how the world works.

Let's discuss.

In Exodus 14, the Hebrew slaves find themselves freed from generations of oppression and abuse. There they stand at the edge of the Red Sea, and the Lord splits the waters and they pass through, fully intact. They've gone from slavery to salvation, and it is a miracle that they escaped, let alone lived to tell the tale. They cross on dry land through the middle of the sea as the waters part, each step bringing them farther from their captors. On the other side of this journey, they are met with a desert, but God provides water for them to drink and bread that appears like magic every morning.

Still, they start to complain about how it doesn't feel like God has a good plan because they don't know where they're going or how they're going to get there. The people of God love a good plan, *amirite*? Finally, in a moment of frustration, one of them says what everyone else has been secretly thinking: "I would rather be a slave back in Egypt because, at least then, I knew what to expect."

We pretend that we'll follow God anywhere when things are clear and easy, but the moment that we hit opposition, we immediately abandon our loyalty to God. We would rather do anything other than be fully vulnerable before God—we have a desire to control even our pain because we suspect that He is not gonna make a good choice. Because let's get real: Vulnerability is absolutely terrifying.

That day with the moving truck, we made it back home. I paid for the gas. And at the end of the day, I texted my pastor, who had been looped into the situation, and thanked him for his encouragement and I told him it had been "humbling."

The next morning, my neighbor came over, and as she sat on the couch, I told her what had happened. And I tried to play it off as almost funny because it made me feel less irresponsible. She went along with it because she is actually kind, but when she left, I suddenly realized that, underneath feeling humbled, I actually felt humiliated.

I came undone. Embarrassment took over all the places I was trying to stake a claim in the Land of Fine. And I wept because I felt like I was everything I never wanted to be. It was Sunday and my church meets in the afternoon, so I got ready slowly, and my hair looked good, and I wore a dress, and as I pulled up to the church building, I realized that I was still trying to *appear* fine. I thought of walking into that church and seeing those friends who had helped me move the day before and humiliation washed over me. I took a seat way back in the corner and softly sobbed through a lot of the sermon, which was about Christ coming near to us even when we're fighting Him. It was about how He heals us. It resonated and made me more upset.

I kind of hated needing to be healed. I hated being present. I hated being found out.

It seems that the story of God's people is one of reluctance to trust that God is safe. Time and time again, they do things because they believe that they know better. It's been in our system since the garden, and something about our sinfulness drives us from trusting God.

This makes sense if you think about it. We are constantly being let down by people: The boyfriend who breaks your heart. The parent who doesn't show up. The spouse who forgets your anniversary. The friend who stands you up. And we have this tendency to assign those experiences to God, too. That He isn't really who He claims to be and isn't to be trusted.

I get this in ways that I couldn't fully explain to you if given a lifetime. But here's the thing, friends: He is safe to draw near to. But to be clear, that doesn't mean what you probably think it does.

Let's go back to the time that my counselor asked if I was angry with God. To that moment when I refused to admit it until I started to cry. The moment when I realized that I have a hard time reconciling the fact that I felt wounded but didn't want God to be in any way part of the pain.

See, in my mind, God is good. But in my heart, I don't know how to face the fact that life is really messy. There are people who would have you believe that we know that God loves us by giving us answers or clarity or peace or happiness. And sometimes, He does do that. But let's *go there* for a moment: What does it say about the character of God when it comes to things being messy or hard or violent or unjust? Does God no longer love us? Is He no longer safe?

I've been walking in these weeks through heartbreak. And I won't go into detail here, but I can say that it has left me feeling raw and confused and I've found God to be a comfort. But at the same time, when I think about the fact that He allowed it in the first place, my chest gets tight. And what comes out of my mouth is, "I thought You were safe."

Safety is a funny thing because we're tempted to believe that safety is comfort. That safety is like a warm blanket that makes you feel calm and tired in a good way. But safety—true safety—isn't exactly that.

My counselor puts it like this: "In order for someone to be safe, they need to be self-aware, have the best intentions, and to act for our good." So if I have a friend and we have a disagreement, and I ask to talk about it and she says, "I don't want to talk right now," that doesn't mean she isn't safe. It means that she knows she's still upset and doesn't want to say something she will regret. And so, with good intentions, she is trying to avoid more grief. And she's a safe person for me to be in a relationship with.

However, if she is fully aware of her anger and has decided to use it to wound me and says, "Yeah, I think we should talk about this right now," so that she can shame me or make me feel small, she is no longer a safe person for me to be in a relationship with. And let me be clear: We sometimes knowingly hurt people. We sometimes manipulate because we want the upper hand, because our understanding of how relationships should actually work is more informed by the kingdom of man than the Kingdom of God. We have to view safety through the right lens, which means we have to acknowledge that it is at times uncomfortable.

Safe doesn't always mean simple.

So when I sit there in counseling, assuming that God isn't safe because He let me get hurt, I'm mistaken. On the contrary, God is fully aware of Himself and the circumstances, He always has the best in mind, and He is moving toward our good, even when we don't realize it.

Here is an example of what I mean: My niece is three years old. She's a tiny version of me, full of sass and laughter. One day she was baking cookies with my sister, and when asked to go wash her hands, she did. She also loves to wear long princess dresses, and in this particular instance, as she was stepping off the stool that she uses to reach the sink, she snagged the edge of her dress. She fell down and got a little goose egg on her forehead.

My sister is a good mom and she comforted her and had her lie down on the couch with a bag of frozen cherries on her forehead to make the swelling go down. But my niece wasn't having it. The bag was cold and her forehead was hurting. So she kept taking it off until my sister finally said in a kind but direct way, "Constance. Keep that bag of cherries on your face."

Constance lay back, full of self-pity, and protested, saying, "You a bad mom."

We laughed at the story later because of the image it conjured of a fussy threenager in a princess dress with a bag of cherries on her face. But at the same time? We do this to God all the dang time.

Constance doesn't realize that the bag of cherries is for her good. That her mama is fully aware, has her best interest in mind, loves her, and wants to do something for Constance's good. But all Constance sees is annoyance and pain and frustration. Does that mean my sister is really a "bad mom"? By no means! We would actually argue that Constance just doesn't have the capacity to see what she doesn't understand, but that doesn't make her assumptions true.

When pain comes and grief is real, we have a God who sits with us in our pain, aware of every part of it, heartbroken with us. And just because it doesn't feel fine or warm or fuzzy, that doesn't mean that He isn't aware or His intention is to harm us. In fact, a lot of people (all of us) deserved punishment and He had mercy. Women were societal outcasts so He put them in key positions in Scripture that dignified them. The prodigal comes home and is welcomed with a party instead of punishment. We have sinned and fallen short, and yet Jesus died on our behalf.

And this is what we need to realize about the Presence

of God: It is our safest option. It's not always the easiest, but it is certainly the safest. Because He is always aware. He is always intending for our best interest, and He is always acting for our good—even when that doesn't fully make sense to us.

....

> And this is what we need to realize about the Presence of God: It is our safest option.

....

Romans 8:28 reminds us that "all things work together for good, for those who are called according to his purpose." And it's easy to hear that and assume it means everything we do will prosper or thrive or be easy. But that's not what it means, per se. What this passage really reminds us of is that we are not the ones in control but God, who is good, is in control and He will work all things together for His good ends and that will be best for us and, therefore, it will be good. Even if it doesn't seem to make sense in the immediate moment. Even when we don't see the end result for years. Even when it's confusing or hard or straight-up humiliating, we know that there are still good things that can come out of it because our God journeys with us through it.

Let's be honest: Some of you read that and thought, *Well, Melissa, you are clearly a big dumb idiot because I don't think it's easy to trust God.* You're not wrong, friend. We're afraid that our plans and His plans don't align. And that if we give Him our dreams, He'll destroy them. If we trust Him with something, He'll take it away. Perhaps it's happened before that you wanted something so badly, but didn't get it. Sometimes later in life we see how these things were actually for our good. But other times, we may not know until eternity what good could come out of them.

I think back to that Sunday I tried so hard to appear fine at church, broken after having to ask my family for help. Communion began and I slowly made my way forward, trying to get a grip. I knelt at the front of the altar and a woman named Beth approached me with the wafers that represent Christ's body. She looked me in the eye and said, "Melissa, this is the body of Christ, broken for you." And I thought about what weight those words and that reality suddenly carried in this small piece of bread. I imagined how a friend recently reminded me that Christ foreknew us, has loved us since before we were born and will love us for all eternity. He knew I would succeed and He knew I would fail miserably but His love remained steadfast nonetheless.

He was fully aware of my bank account when I thought I had it together. He was 100 percent sure that I was going to lose it all, and yet, He continued to walk toward me. There, in the distance, like when He came out to His disciples on the surface of the water, it was as if I could make out the shape of His figure moving slowly toward me. With grace and understanding, when I didn't want to be actually present for fear of being known in my shortcomings, He drew near.

I took the bread, and as the cup passed by me, I dipped in my wafer as the words "the blood of Christ, poured out for many" were whispered over me. This love is not just for myself but for all of us.

Every week, I take communion. Every week the bread is handed to me and is dipped into the wine. Every week, it is slowly swallowed and the tiniest burn of those two flavors shocks my taste buds. But this week, the shock of it went down deep into my bones in some way, and as the flavor shocked my taste buds, it shocked my whole being as if to say, "I'm here." He felt near, even in my mess, and I felt safe. It was a surprise to feel so loved on a day when I could barely look at myself, overwhelmed by embarrassment. Suddenly, I valued the Presence of Jesus because He was the only one I wasn't ashamed to show my face around. And it made all the difference.

I took a few breaths and pushed myself back up to my feet and took a seat near a friend. No longer ashamed, I sat in sore gratitude as we sang the words *"There's gonna be a great rejoicing."* And my mind went back to the great anchor that keeps me steady: Christ's Presence is always for our good. His nearness is always to bring healing. We come as we are and we are found out, for better and for worse.

In my running and racing, my performing and trying to be *fine*; in my distraction, my uncertainty, and my desire to keep up appearances; when I am a responsible adult, or when bad things happen and I feel like the opposite, I have a God who is ever-present. A God who doesn't just sit in the same room as me or tolerate me only when I'm meeting His standards. Rather, He sees right into my very soul and the part of my life I'd like to keep covered, and He pulls up a chair.

He sees me sitting back with my legs and arms crossed, distracted by a thousand other things, and He puts both feet on the floor, inviting me to do the same. I slowly lean forward and stare at the floor until I look up and see Him there, with kindness in His eyes. My phone is getting text messages but I've somehow managed to get it to be totally silent and this is where I am certain this story has to start.

The consequence of the Presence of God is that we are found. We are seen and known, and instead of that being the stuff of nightmares, it becomes our home.

> The consequence of the Presence of God is that we are found. We are seen and known, and instead of that being the stuff of nightmares, it becomes our home.

The Presence of God is our good. It is for our best. It is our security. And when we take the time to seek it out, it manages to find us pretty easily. In how we pick up children and how we shake hands with new neighbors. In the changing of seasons and the slicing of a sandwich in two. In the laughter of my nieces who are pretending to be puppies and in the late nights in the office—He is present. In all of it.

Perhaps you're like me and you fear being known because it means that all of you is seen, even the ugly parts. Perhaps you have been told since you were young that in order to be loved you have to have your things in order. Let me tell you this: Christ is here, whether you want Him to be or not. He is closer than your eyelashes when you blink, nearer than the breath on your lips, and He's not going anywhere.

This is the tension that we are forced to reckon with. I call it: being a human person. His ways are not our ways and He knows every single condition that had led to this moment. So maybe you don't get the job you wanted but the person who does is blessed by the income. Maybe your car gets totaled but you meet a new friend on the bus. Large or small, clear or muddled, we can rest in the knowledge that He is aware and His intentions are best and He is working for our good.

Sandra McCracken puts it like this in her song "Fool's Gold": *if it's not okay, then it is not the end.*

* * *

We often try to distance ourselves from God because we believe that He's not going to follow through on His promise. In Psalm 62, the psalmist is waiting for the Lord and declares a trust in Him. That word there for trust? It's been translated as "to put confidence in something" or—get this—"unsuspecting."

I *say* that I trust God with things, but do I really have no suspicion when He does things I don't fully understand? No. I get crazy suspicious. And I'll admit to you here: I sometimes think that "trusting" God is begrudgingly, only technically, letting Him steer. As if I held the wheel to begin with, I say things like, "God, you can have this" or "God, I give you control."

Do we really believe that He's looking for us to hand things over to Him? Do we think that the Creator needs some kind of permission from His created beings? I don't think so. He's mighty and sovereign—which means He's already got the wheel firmly in hand.

There are moments when we experience the mercy and kindness of God in powerful ways, but it is easy to forget, we have to be reminded, and we have to preach it to ourselves so that when we start to lose our grip, we have something to recall and bring to mind.

It turns out that one of the most honest things we can actually bring to Him is our trust. Our hearts that say, "I believe that you have *got this*," even when it feels impossible. We can confess in our creeds and journal entries and conversations and songs and letters that our hearts long, deep down, after His goodwill. That we want to be aligned to what He has in mind and see the bigger pictures He is painting with no caveats. No conditions. No suspicion.

In Mark 9:24, a man cries out to Jesus, "I believe; help

my unbelief!" and isn't that just the way? We're constantly needing His help to believe when all is lost or we feel found out or humiliated or our sin comes back to bite us.

Oh, that we would be a people who are strong in confidence, entirely unsuspecting of the motives of our good God. And until we become those people, may we keep asking Him to help our unbelief.

God has proven over and over again that He would come for His people. He freed them from slavery and led them through the desert—even when they shouted in protest that they'd rather be slaves. He carried them and fought for them and pursued them both as a collective people and as individuals. And then He provided for them with Jesus—God with us. Always making a way to be close to us so that we might know Him and His goodness.

Ephesians 2:1–3 reminds us of our condition with and without Christ.

And you were dead in the trespasses and sins in which you once walked, following the course of this world, following the prince of the power of the air, the spirit that is now at work in the sons of disobedience—among whom we all once lived in the passions of our flesh, carrying out the desires of the body and the mind, and were by nature children of wrath, like the rest of mankind.

Now let's zoom in on some of this: We were dead. Not even super sick or feeling a little gross. We were totally, completely, no-pulse dead. Why? Because of our sins. The inheritance of our world and fallenness. We all were in the depths of sin and desolation, distant from God. Let's continue along in the passage, though:

> *But God, being rich in mercy, because of the great love with which he loved us, even when we were dead in our trespasses, made us alive together with Christ—by grace you have been saved—and raised us up with him and seated us with him in the heavenly places in Christ Jesus, so that in the coming ages he might show the immeasurable riches of his grace in kindness toward us in Christ Jesus. (2:4–7)*

That section started with a discussion around the word *agape*. We've seen that word *agape* before—the Greek word for LOVE. It has to do with an unrelenting, always-enduring, covenant love. The Hebrew equivalent? You guessed it, you little theologian you—*chesed*. That everlasting Love that comes from God alone. That "I'll-move-heaven-and-earth-to-get-close-to-you-even-when-you-mess-up-and-fall-short-and-run-away" love. He took that love, and because of it, He didn't just make things better—He brought the dead to life again.

Why would we withhold our trust from a safe God who loves us like that?

When we see God as He really is—fully aware, intending the best, working for good—we see that He is safe. And when we recall the narrative of His people and His character that pursues us not just for kicks, but because He deeply loves us and would do anything—and has done everything—to care for us well, we suddenly see who we are dealing with. A God who is safe when relationships fail. A God who is good when the world is broken. A God who is worth trusting when the future is uncertain. A God who welcomes us into His Presence without shame or humiliation.

May we run to him, knowing that He has always run after us.

CHAPTER FIVE

Our Work Matters

When I was probably thirteen years old, I got my first job that paid me for something other than babysitting or feeding the neighbors' dog while they were on vacation. It was at a pet store nearly twenty-five minutes away and my mom dropped me off. I put on an actual dog costume and stood on the corner with a sign for the grand opening of All Star Pets. It was summer in California, so it had to be nearly 100 degrees, but I was so excited to have a job that I didn't really mind. I got paid about 50 dollars in cash for probably six hours of work, which to a thirteen-year-old was a *solid deal.*

My first formal job, once I was old enough to be put on a payroll, was at a little golf shop in our small town. I talked to people about putters and sweater material and what kind of golf ball was best for how they played the game. I was there for two years and then got a job at a bookstore until I moved to Chicago for college. In college, I was an editor at the student paper. In grad school, I worked in the marketing office. And then, I took a job in Texas as a paid intern for a Christian nonprofit.

These early jobs involved things that I loved: golf,

books, writing, and communications. And they were also in areas that I was gifted in, which made them all the more enjoyable. But even the best jobs that I have had come with not-so-awesome experiences, like customers who are upset, people who think you don't know what you're talking about, and readers who disagree. These jobs I had, like any job, came with hazards.

As I've gotten older and embedded myself further and further into the workforce, I've realized that it's much more complicated than we tend to believe. Sometimes we do jobs we love. Sometimes, we do jobs we hate. We go to school or train for vocations. We get put on disability or medical leave. We get fired or we quit, we get hired or we take a sabbatical. Some people get paid too much and others nowhere near enough. Much of our adult lives tends to revolve around vocation in ways that transcend culture and language.

It's actually woven deep into the fabric of our culture in ways that are so obvious that they often go unnoticed. From childhood, we ask kids what they want to be when they grow up. As twenty-somethings, we "join the work force" and dream of retirement from our thirties on, waiting for that moment when we can be done and really enjoy our lives. Work takes over much of our conversations and seems to be at the forefront of so many hours of weeks, but at the same time, we don't often grapple with what vocation represents and how it shapes us.

If I told you that I listen to one band for eight hours a day and even sometimes into the night, you can be certain that I would be influenced by it. By the lyrics and the tempo and the culture that it represents. If it were angry music, I might have a hard time finding peace. If it were slow music, I might have a hard time getting excited. Our work influences us and shapes us, but if we don't have a great handle on what it is and why it matters and how it moves us, we won't be able to pull from it and put into it what we were created to glean and contribute.

A few chapters back, we talked about creation. About how God created everything in kingdoms and filled those kingdoms with kings. The narrative of this beautiful reality was ruined by sin, but the world God created still exists. Man and woman are placed in the garden and commanded to tend it and care for it and protect it and cultivate it. They are given good and holy work to do. To make the world better than it was yesterday. This process was the first job, really. Mankind was made to work before sin entered the world, which means that it is a good and God-ordained thing for us to do work.

Sometimes we get to see that when we nail a presentation or tackle a big project or get an encouraging review. We feel like we know our stuff and walk away from the office or the shop or the classroom with a deep sense of accomplishment. When we want to share something we've made or tell our spouse or parents about something that "happened at work today," it's something worth celebrating.

But we have to remember that work has been complicated by the fall, too. Everything broke, remember?

Some people make money by exploiting others. Some people get trafficked by those who have an enticing, but entirely fake, job offer for them. Some people get paid to do horrible things to other people. Some people are treated unfairly by their co-workers or gossiped about behind their backs. Some workplaces feel like a never-ending cycle of boredom and pretending you're not on social media when the boss comes around the corner. The system of the workplace is flawed and far from what it was created to be. It's far from what God intended it to do.

··

See, everything that we do, in word
or deed or thought, will do one of
four things. It will expose, explain,
exhort, or exploit.

··

The motives that we carry are going to flow through our actions, whether we willingly let them or not. Friendships can be used to manipulate someone into getting what you want. Education can be turned into brainwashing. Sarcasm turns encouragement into an emotional hand grenade, aimed to destroy. But at the same time, seeking answers can turn into understanding. And a simple act can bring someone's weary heart to life. Telling the truth can expose the lies that we believe.

We have a choice in how we come at everything, and we have to protect our motives and orient them toward the

Creator, or we will easily—far too easily—fall into the trap of taking something beautiful and ruining it.

God has always valued work. It makes the world around us work, and it helps us to do things together to make the world better. Remember the "cultivate and keep" command I mentioned earlier? Well, it's still what we are called to do. It just may not look like gardening or farming. Instead, we go to meetings, write papers, tell stories, play music, serve food, prepare meals, restock shelves, and raise children.

The work of cultivating and keeping has a whole lot to do with God's heart for nourishing life, beauty, and remaking things into better things. When we walk into a situation and make it richer than it was, it's a form of cultivation.

Unfortunately, we have a tendency to forget that. We start to use a hierarchy for how we view jobs and adopt the mind-set of the world around us. We forget what kingdom we are trying to build, and in doing so, we lose vision. We decide that if you're serving food at a high price, it makes you more valuable than someone working in the fast-food industry. Or if someone's a preschool teacher, they're less important than a college professor. Both are feeding and serving. Both are building and making things new. Both are encouraging and teaching.

In a lively conversation on Facebook today, I asked my friends if anyone could think of a job that's legal (i.e., a hit-man would be disqualified) that doesn't benefit society. The list was sarcastic and silly. People were getting really specific, such as "real estate shark" or "professional gambler," and then my friend Jim chimed in with, "I mean, writing or owning a business is not categorically bad, but there are simply bad ways to use those skills. It is pretty hard to think of a vocation that's categorically unhelpful."

Jesus Himself had a job as a carpenter for years before He began His ministry. He called disciples as they were working as fishermen. The writers of the Gospels were doctors and lawyers. And yet God uses every profession to bring Himself glory when it's oriented toward Him. You don't have to be in full-time ministry to encounter the living God and do His work, friends.

We see this play out in daily life, even today. I think of the nurse at the doctor's office when I lived in Texas. I had mentioned that I was working in ministry and she told me she was a believer. This small moment ended up creating a trust that went deeper than normal conversation with the nurse at a doctor's office because I knew we shared faith. I was scared because I'd been having troubling symptoms and we'd been unable to find the cause. One afternoon, sitting in the exam room, she looked at me and said, "I promise we're going to figure this out, even if it takes weeks or months. I won't let it take months. It's like when Scripture says we see things dimly but one day we'll have clarity. One day, we will figure this out."

Her words gave me comfort and hope, even after a diagnosis that wasn't good. I knew that there was someone in that fearful and uncertain place that represented faith and surety and who was bringing me before the throne when I was nearly too weak to stand. She acted as a caregiver not just physically, but spiritually. This isn't a new concept in my life. I've had teachers who poured into me outside of class. I've had co-workers become some of my closest friends and tell me the truth when I didn't want to hear it. There are always opportunities to use our work to point others to the Truth of Jesus, even if our work isn't overtly religious.

That's one of the best things about the Kingdom of God: We can see it in everything and we can help God build it in all the contexts that we find ourselves in. It's in silent prayers prayed for our struggling clients. It's in helpful insight or advice that you offer to your employee who is at a crossroads. It's in the way that you interact with your flight attendants when you're traveling. It's in the way that you comfort your child who has fallen off their bike. It's in the way you prepare a meal or extend an invitation or listen to someone.

We have a tendency to pull apart our vocation from our passion. For example, someone may say that their greatest passion is painting. Maybe since they were a child they wanted to be the next Van Gogh, but as time went on, they majored in accounting and painting fell by the wayside. Since it wasn't paying the bills, it was not worth pursuing. And there's this ache, right? To be able to do what you love and still survive. Cinema is full of examples of a child with big aspirations who goes against their family's expectations in order to live out a lifelong dream. We elevate this story and it's an important one: You should do what you love to do and are gifted at doing.

However. Sometimes we imagine a dream job and assume that if we don't immediately get to do that or if circumstances start to prohibit it from happening, we are failures. We take it right to our identity and gifts and assume that we are doomed not to live out our passion. Now, I want to speak directly to the concerns I believe a few of you may hold.

First, to the twenty-somethings who are making their way in the world: Adulting is hard—I get that. If I can get *really* honest, I've had to hold off on buying groceries twice in the last year because my checking account was in single digits. I've done the "live without air-conditioning because it saves money, even though it's eighty-five degrees in the house in the summertime" thing. I have been an intern who made coffee or ran around the city with a backpack of camera equipment, trying to get one good shot, or spent late hours trying to complete a mountain of tasks. I get that the struggle is crazy real.

We grew up being told by the media around us that we could be anything we wanted—but no one told us that it would take some serious time and discipline. No one said, "But first, you have to pay your dues." So I'm here to tell you: We gotta pay our dues. These are not years that you get to waste because you're frustrated that you aren't *making it*. These are not years you get to dismiss because *you'll figure it out when you get your life together*. These are not years to throw away because you aren't getting what you want.

These are the years of forming habits that will dictate how you finish well one day. These are years of work that you sometimes don't want to do because it'll prepare you for something else later. These are years of cultivating a sense of purpose even in the things you don't love about your career at this moment. If He can use shepherds and fishermen and those who were considered to have lame jobs to bring about His purposes, He can use you, too. These are the years of development—good or bad. The habits that you form and practice will follow you, for better or for worse. Learn to cheer for your co-workers and not treat them like competition. Learn to respect your boss and not talk behind her or his back. Learn to be honest, even if it means you don't impress everyone all the time.

Second, I want to talk to those of you who might feel like you've lost a dream because of something else. Maybe you didn't finish school or you suffered an injury that ended a promising career. Maybe you came upon hard times that left you in dire need of a *filler job* that turned into a thirty-year career. Or maybe you made the decision to stay home with your kids, even though you went to college for something totally unlike parenting.

Your gifts were given to you by God and He intends for you to use them, just maybe not how you imagined right now. Maybe you're good with people or great at organization or excellent at seeing the long view. And maybe, in your life right now, this looks like leading a small group or a book club. Maybe this looks like helping overwhelmed friends clean out their closets without judging them or making them feel small. Maybe it looks like helping young people plan ahead and choose the slow, steady path in a world that's telling them to "Go, go, go!"

Just because you aren't being paid by someone to do what you were made to do doesn't mean you weren't made to do it. Carly Bannister says it this way in a song sung from the perspective of God: "For the rest of your life, you'll never regret chasing the things that you love. And maybe the crowds won't chant your name, but I'll be right there all along, saying, 'Well done.'"

....

> Just because you aren't being paid by someone to do what you were made to do doesn't mean you weren't made to do it.

....

God is not up in heaven scoffing at the small ways that the Kingdom is being built—He is delighted by them. He has given us work to do, and whether or not the "right people" acknowledge it is neither here nor there because guess what? They're just people. And they're flawed and probably not as perfect as you imagine them to be. When we lose focus of whose Kingdom we are building, we start to believe the lie that He hasn't truly gifted us, and in order to be legitimate, we have to prove our worth.

There is work that we must do, yes. And it's not always a laugh a minute. But he's also given us unique callings and abilities. Scripture reminds us that we are like different parts of a body. We're not all the eyes, the hands, or the legs. But we are all needed, and Ephesians reminds us that "when each part is working properly, it makes the body grow so that it builds itself up in love" (4:16). And that's an important thing to consider: We have to be working properly. We cannot squelch our gifts. We need not use them only in the most popular and elevated ways in order for them to matter. But we have to use them.

You never know how using your gifts might influence those around you. Each of us is born with a unique skill set that we get to use for the Kingdom. Some of us write, others sing, some draw, build, calculate, administer, or organize. Every gift is important and we need one another to thrive. Just because what you can do well isn't glamorous doesn't mean it doesn't matter.

So if you're in that place of not wanting to develop your gifts, even in small ways, I want you to know that we need you not to give up. We need you to build your corner of the Kingdom, regardless of if you're being paid in a formal, full-time job or not. You can be an accountant who cooks, or a stay-at-home mom who writes, or an engineer who plays guitar on Sundays at church. Because when we use those skills and pursue those gifts, we are partaking in the cultivation and keeping of the world around us. And honestly? There are no small parts.

My first job out of seminary was a dream. I got to work for an incredible ministry and hear stories regularly about how God was transforming the lives of women around the world. I got to research for Bible studies and make promo videos and plan social media. I was also in Austin, Texas, where the food is unparalleled. But right before I went, someone said something to me that stuck in my head and made me consider what has to be one of the most common fears we have: *What if they don't like me?*

I knew that I was coming from an academic background and I wasn't particularly on-brand. Also, I don't wear makeup and I was moving to Texas. So I resolved to do the hard work of ministry and let myself enjoy very little of it. I decided that I would just be good at the nerdy, behind-the-scenes stuff and it would be my ticket to belonging. I figured that one can't be unwanted if they show up early and stay late and think very little of themselves. It was a false humility that was really more of a self-punishing than anything else.

Instead of enjoying the freedom of the time between graduation and this job, I decided right before I left to take Greek over the summer to better prepare. When I moved there, I resolved to put my head down and do my job well, but I did it at the cost of something else: my identity. I believed that if I poured myself unrelentingly into this work, which was good work, I would be able to earn the affection of other people. I used the excuse of being an off-brand, non-Austinite seminarian and said, "Well, they probably think that I won't fit in because of my background, so I'll just gain their respect for other things where I socially lack." I didn't want to be fully myself for fear of social rejection, so I worked harder for those I wanted to befriend more. We do this in the workplace all the time—we've got the job, but we want to secure our standing in some way. They surely can't reject me if I'm doing my job above and beyond all the time, right?

We sometimes see our work as a constant performance review, and it's easy to push so hard into that lie that we let it become our identity. And it wasn't that I saw myself as only my work, but I considered my work to be the most important thing about me. And because I didn't have good boundaries, I said "yes" to everything, later realizing that doing so is an easy way to burn yourself out even further.

Let me be clear here: I largely did this to myself. No one was telling me to come in early or stay late, but I believed that I had to go hard all the time to make up for the fact that I wasn't sure where I fit. There was always an excuse that I made for myself to those around me who asked if I was overtired. I'd say, "We just have an unexpected project," or "I'm planning on resting tomorrow." What I really would have said if I were being honest would be, "I'm afraid that if I don't prove myself, I'll be alone."

In college, my friend Hannah had a Post-it Note on her desk that I must have passed a hundred times as we lingered around the dorms. But it wasn't until our senior year that I actually stopped to read it. There, in her curvy handwriting, it said, *Busyness is not a badge.*

I paused and considered that for a moment. In my own

pursuit of acceptance, I had hurried everywhere, and had done *all the things*, and had cared about every cause. I cultivated an understanding of current issues, topics, problems, and solutions, and I bounded from event to event and from class to class, acquiring more knowledge, making more lunch dates, planning more parties, and believing that as long as the plates kept spinning, I was killing the game.

Busyness was my badge. And my history of busyness went back even further as I thought about it more: I'd been a varsity athlete, a member of three choirs, and had played a leadership role in fifteen clubs by my senior year. Yes, I was a pro at *busy*. I know what you're thinking: *But there are only five days in a school week. How were you in fifteen clubs?*

Let's see, there was Choir Council, Christian Club, Interact, Red Cross Club, and Key Club—for which I was the regional oversight, so I had a relationship with eleven schools' clubs. I was literally joined to clubs at schools that I didn't even go to. I was on the varsity golf team, I did pitching statistics for the varsity baseball team, and church was a whole other thing. I was on the music team, I helped with tech, and I was a leader for the junior high ministry.

Sometimes, when we aren't sure where our identity lies and what our place is, we just try to be part of all of them. We assume that if doing one thing is a good idea, doing everything must increase worth and legitimacy. You can't argue about music with the choir achiever or about health with the Red Cross Club founder, or about service with the member of twelve service clubs, or about faith with the ministry leader. And it wasn't that I really wanted to be an authority, I just wanted to be right and to know something.

Whether I had intended it or not, I was creating a life pattern that would try to ruin me. It was a tendency to overstretch my schedule and to overcommit my efforts. It was a habit of running out of gas in my car because I didn't have the time or resources to keep it on full. It was the hankering for more pins in my letterman jacket and more signatures in my yearbook. And the saddest part is that I didn't even know that I was doing these things for reasons that were sad and unhealthy.

So I became the photographer for the marching band.

It's been this way from the start. My parents were going to name me Sarah Elizabeth but got into a disagreement when I was born because I showed up with my dad's darker coloring and he felt that the name wasn't Hispanic enough. They changed it to Melissa, which means *honeybee*, and when I was a kid, a family friend used to refer to me as a busy bee. I guess that tendency of mine just never stopped. My actual name is one of hurry and flitting from thing to thing.

My quick-moving interests were, in reality, the result of a combination of anxiety and misplaced identity. I had titles and leadership roles, but while it was my job to *pour out* into all of these activities and the people involved, I didn't know how to let myself be *poured into*. I struggled with a lack of affirmation in my actual gifts and in who I was as someone who is loved by Christ. I just kept pushing through, pretending that I didn't need the encouragement of others. I wasn't being told the truth about who I was and what Jesus wanted in a way that actually made sense to me. My assumption was that if I was leading, I knew what I was doing. My plan to appear put together, in that way, worked. But since it wasn't true that I knew what I was doing, I was left isolated, and so I did what anyone else would do: I kept my mouth shut about my own issues and helped others solve theirs instead. I longed for affirmation, so I poured out kind words to others constantly.

At the time, my confidence and hope and life were built upon things other than Jesus and the love He was already offering. They were built upon achievement and titles and honors and certificates. When faced with a moment of insecurity, what I needed was to stop and turn around and look Him in the eye and whisper, "But who do you say I am?" I needed to tuck away into a corner of the room and close my eyes and let Him tell me the truth. I needed to open my Bible and soak in it, instead of opening it to come up with all the answers. My relationship with Jesus was like dating someone for rides to school, or marrying someone for help with getting things off the top shelf that I can't reach by myself.

But here's the thing about a relationship with someone based on how they can make your life better: Eventually, you realize that you'll never be satisfied, and they'll never be in the place of intimacy that they have to be in for this whole thing to work, because you won't be honest or vulnerable. You'll keep taking things back, and texting to tell them you're on the way when you haven't left yet, and making excuses for why you don't have time to stop and look them in the eye.

You'll wonder why you're tired and why things feel like they take too much effort, and when you yell for someone to answer the phone, you'll realize that no one is going to do that because you've managed to tell everyone to leave because you can do it yourself. When you make yourself play every role, there's nothing left for anyone else.

I wish that someone had told me that the world was going to work just fine without my constant achievement. I wish they had told me that if I dropped one ball, the apocalypse wasn't going to happen. I wish they had taken the sponge out of my hand and told me to go sit down while they finished loading the dishwasher. But we live in a world where achievement is so worshipped that no one would have done that because it would have seemed like a punishment. And let's get real: I wouldn't have let them take the proverbial sponge because if I don't load the dishwasher on top of everything else, I don't have the right to be tired.

We often believe that being tired is a sign that you're a hard worker. And while that's true after a literal marathon, or giving birth, or moving into a new house, I'm not so sure it's what we should aim to feel consistently. I exhausted myself so often that I actually couldn't tell the difference between feeling tired and being straight-up weary.

Enter Jesus.

"Come to me, all who are weary and heavy laden, and I

will give you a list of three more things to do," said Jesus never.

Rather, He sees me standing there and won't break eye contact as He reaches around and unties my apron and puts out His hand asking for the sponge. I refuse. He gently puts His hands on my shoulders and turns me toward the living room. I make excuses. He walks me to the couch. I begin to slowly shake my head from side to side and my eyes start to sting. He nods a "yes" and sits me down across from Himself as He sits on the coffee table. We are knee to knee and I feel my inner achiever start to come undone. I sit there, water dripping on the floor from the soapy sponge I can't seem to hand over. He takes my hands and I lean into Him, my forehead on His shoulder, and start to cry.

"If I stop, I won't matter anymore," I confess.

"If you stop," He says, "we can get down to what actually matters."

The story of finding our place in the vocational landscape of the Kingdom of God has a lot more to do with stripping away than building our résumé of achievements. There's a reason that when someone stands up and says, "I don't know how to reconcile what I love and what I do for a living," most of the room says, "Welcome to the club. Try to figure it out on the weekends."

••

The story of finding our place in the
vocational landscape of the Kingdom
of God has a lot more to do with
stripping away than building our
résumé of achievements.

••

After I finished my time in Austin, with the job I'd put
my identity into, I moved to Nashville. I got a job where I
went in early and stayed late. I left that job unexpectedly,
and a few weeks after settling into a new, less hectic job,
my friend Sandra remarked, "You seem happier." I told her
that I was.

"You know," she said, "when you work too much, everything is important."

She's right. When we focus only on our job, we start
to care about every detail like our reputations depend on
them, because in our minds, they do.

One afternoon, about a year ago, I got a phone call from
my friend Jenn. We had met when I was living in Austin
and she knew I could take photos and video. She and another gal named Kelly had started this thing called The
Well Studio, a place for dreamers and doers to come together and figure out how to live out their calling in the
company of one another. They'd just launched a facet of
it called Camp Well the year before, and from what I'd
seen, it looked straight *dreamy*. Four days of a retreat in a

beautiful location with like-minded women who were doing awesome things. I'd wanted to go but didn't know if I'd
belong there.

Jenn explained on the call that they'd wanted me to do
some photos and video in exchange for a ticket. I agreed
but had no idea how much it would change everything.
I'd done a ton of these kinds of women's events before, as
a photographer or videographer, and so as I prepared, I
assumed it would be a normal *job* where I stayed on the
fringes. That was my most comfortable place—cheering
for everyone else and not really participating. When the
time for the event rolled around, I flew into the Denver
Airport and rented a car. As I drove two hours into the
mountains, I started to get nervous for a few reasons.
First, I had lost phone reception and for forty-five minutes
straight had been following handwritten directions toward
the remote location. I managed to figure out the way to a
nine-mile dirt road that led to my destination, Lost Valley
Ranch. Second, I didn't really know what to expect.

Once I got there, I did what I always do: I offered to
over-help with tasks in addition to my own responsibili-
ties, and I didn't fully engage as an equal. Women talked
about community and how hard it is to be alone in what
you're doing. And the profound thing was that they built
a little tribe right there, stepping in to pray, cheer, encourage, and speak life over one another. There was no
competition nor performance nor desire to prove themselves as better than anyone else. At Camp Well, we use
the term "Dream Defender" to describe this. We take four

days and we fight for truth and beauty and relationship. And to me, it's the clearest image of what it means to live out vocation in the Kingdom. Some women come with a company they're starting or a dream they need to brainstorm, or they even come in the middle of grieving a dream lost, but everyone walks away refreshed and refocused, because they pull apart all the extra nonsense about platform and engagement and numbers and replace it with the Word of God and prayer.

I loved what they were doing, but at first didn't feel like I could give myself permission to belong. I certainly cheered for everyone else in the room, but I wasn't there as a participant, in my own mind, and up to that point no one had noticed. Until, that is, I met Andee.

Andee is this girl with an incredible work ethic who says exactly what she means. She's Jenn's cousin and we met in the back room, setting up welcome bags for the first session. Something about her struck me, and I couldn't figure out what or why until the second night at camp. We were waiting for some women to leave a room so we could reset it with the next morning's table décor, and it was getting later and later. Both of us resolved to be sleep deprived but do our job, so we sat on a couch downstairs until the ladies were done having a heart-to-heart conversation.

She asked me a bit about myself and I answered in the ways I always do, letting her glimpse some of the honesty and darkness then following it up with a bit of light-heartedness. She looked at me with sincerity and without hesitation and said, "You cover up your insecurity with humor, don't you?"

Andee had seen right through me and I knew that I'd been found out. I didn't know what to do with that kind of kindness mixed with honesty. I'd watched women wrestle with their own identity and calling, wondering what to do next, and there I was, getting a taste of what it might mean to have someone care enough to walk that out with me. She didn't accept me because of the job I was doing, but the person that I was.

Since that night, Andee has become one of my dearest friends, rejoicing when I rejoice and mourning when I mourn. She has been kind and honest and loyal and supportive—more a sister than a friend. Her friendship saw past what I had to offer (because Andee is the kind of gal who is not impressed by fanfare), and she gave me the permission I needed to admit that I was more than my camera or my pen. It was the start of what would be a long road to freedom, which we'll talk about in the next chapter.

When it comes to vocation, it's okay for things to feel complicated. And it's okay for us to feel torn between what we do for our nine-to-five and what brings us the most joy. But my prayer is that we would not worship either so much that we base our actual worth upon it. You are not your vocation. You are not your calling. You are not your dreams. You are not what you achieve. Rather, you are a soul who was created by God to do specific things.

We are reminded that "we are His workmanship, created

in Christ Jesus for good works, which God prepared beforehand, that we should walk in them" (Ephesians 2:10).

Wherever you find yourself, and in whatever job you do, you have been made to do it with the gifts He has given you. It's not an accident that you have the skills that others do not. And it's not an accident that others have abilities that you lack. He knows what He's doing, and you have a purpose in every moment, in every action, and in every task. Use those opportunities to build the Kingdom—it's what you were created to do, for the glory of God and the good of others.

••

Wherever you find yourself, and in whatever job you do, you have been made to do it with the gifts He has given you.

••

CHAPTER SIX

On Being Known

The fundamental idea that God sees us and uniquely speaks to each of us seems simple enough, but this was the chapter that did me in. For the last few days, I haven't stopped crying over the fullness of this reality, in both good and bad ways. A lot of these chapters feel like lessons learned that I am thrilled to share with others, but this may be the one that still feels a little like trying to pick up a dropped bar of soap, sliding through my fingers every time I think I have a good grip. It feels nearest, but somehow the hardest to look in the eye.

Part of what makes this chapter weighty right now is probably the fact that the Presence of God in our individual stories is perhaps the place that most of us are wounded in some way. We have lived long enough to endure some very real heartbreak and we wonder if maybe He took an afternoon off when we got the call, or the accident happened. We feel like God seems to speak to everyone else in meaningful ways, but there's this haunting feeling that overcomes us as we consider the perceived void around a moment of pain or need.

Wounded by the struggle of our stories, we assume that

God may not be exactly who He says He is. That He may be in theory speaking to other people, but He probably doesn't want to carry on a conversation with us. Or if He does, it's merely an obligation. There's small talk but nothing that involves saying something with enough depth that you'd have to pause to hold back honest tears.

There are two ways that we splinter our understanding and experience of God. First, we know Him in a strictly intellectual way based on some stories or encounters that other people may have with Him. The testimony of others is good enough for us, and we lack an intimacy with Jesus that we've only heard about. We think to ourselves, *Wow, that kind of close encounter with God sounds great, but I don't know if I could really believe it in my own life.* We sometimes have the idea that God certainly works in specific ways in other people's lives, but He doesn't move in our own. Whether consciously or not, we see that kind of potential for closeness with Him as a distant knowledge that we struggle to believe on a personal level.

The other way that we splinter from Him comes not from a lack of opportunities to know God, but from the feeling that He had a chance and just didn't take it. This is commonly because of something that we've faced in the past. We don't have a close relationship with God because it seems that when we were hoping to be seen by Him, we didn't even notice His Presence, let alone His affection. And as time goes on, we decide that He must not actually be paying any attention. But out of loyalty to our faith, we believe every other part of the gospel—just not the part where we are uniquely embraced and seen and valued. Not the part where you sense His nearness in moments of significance and ordinariness. We don't see His glory in the sunlight that bounces off the kitchen sink or the endless waves of the ocean. His kindness is not felt in moments of loss or grief. His comfort is not something you sense when you call out to Him. Instead, your words echo into a void, and after you go hoarse, you stop calling out.

We tell ourselves this particular story a lot of the time because it's the most human. If you call a friend in a time of desperation and she doesn't answer, you try again, and if she never calls you back, she must not be the kind of person you can be close with. We call on God, and when we are met with uncomfortable silence, we come to the conclusion that He isn't up to returning our calls—not even so much as a text message.

For this, my heart breaks for you. For the pain you have known, I am truly sorry. Perhaps the hardest part of writing this chapter is that I have countless faces flashing across my mind of dearly loved friends who have had this exact experience. I have sat with them and wept over their pain and it is not something that you just *get over*. It's a deep ache that follows us around from morning to evening and all through the night. I have found myself in these moments and they still linger in my mind whenever a new pain arises. Grief has a way of calling to mind previous grief, and the more it happens, the longer it takes to process through.

The voice of God or its silence are mysteries we don't

get to fully understand on this side of eternity. In order to get the big picture of how God speaks, we need to start with a few basics. In Scripture, God's Presence and insight show up in two big ways: general revelation and special revelation. General revelation is for everyone. It's things like the beauty of a sunset or the fact that we have the Word of God in our hands. It's something that impacts everyone in a general way that points to the Creator and His majesty. Special revelation is a unique moment in Scripture where someone encounters God. This would be something like the burning bush that Moses saw in the wilderness or the way the sea was split in two. These are special revelations that happen for an individual person or a specific group of people.

One of the hallmarks of God's character, in fact, is the reality that He speaks to us at all. When I say "speaks," I mean communicates the truth of who He is. It's not like there's an audible voice telling us new information. The way God speaks is often through means outside Himself, but it always is true to what Scripture reveals. If you believe that God is telling you to cause needless division or gossip or spread malicious lies, it isn't God speaking because those things go against Scripture. When God speaks to us, He does not contradict His own character.

So what does it mean to experience God in a personal way? One of my favorite examples is found in the Book of Ruth. Although it's only four chapters long, I've spent a lot of time in this book over the last ten years, translating it from Hebrew for classes and digging deeper into the implications of its narrative.

Ruth was a Moabitess, which means she was a woman from the land of Moab. This was a country near Israel. A man named Elimelech is the main character at the start of this story. Everything seems to revolve around him as the patriarch of a family that finds themselves in a tough situation. Elimelech, his wife Naomi, and their two sons, Mahlon and Chilion, decide to go to find food because of a famine that has hit Israel. They are from Bethlehem, and they travel to Moab in the hopes of a better future. And then, Elimelech dies.

Back in the Ancient Near East, men were the providers for their family. All of the family's financial, social, and relational security was tied to his work and provision. Therefore, when Elimelech dies, his wife is left not only grieving but in need of practical help. Luckily, she still has her sons. The sons then become the focus, and the story tells us that they take wives who are from Moab. For ten years, they live with their wives, Orpah and Ruth. For ten years, they are sojourning and making their way in Moab. Things seem to have returned, at least partially, to normal. Naomi is taken care of; her sons are married; all is well. And then, Mahlon and Chilion die.

The focus of the story shifts to the woman—Naomi. As the passage says, "The woman was left without her two sons and her husband" (Ruth 1:5).

Devastating. Heartbreaking. Terrifying. Naomi has no one left to help her. The reason that Scripture wants us to care for the orphans and widows is because they were culturally the most vulnerable. Naomi has been left without anyone to protect her.

At this point, she hears that there is food again in Israel, so she decides to go back. She had heard that God had been providing crops, and so she goes where the action is. Still in mourning, she sets out with her two daughters-in-law. But Naomi is hurting and doesn't want any more pain for the daughters-in-law, so she insists that they go back home to Moab. They're still young enough to remarry. They tell her that they want to stay with her, but she tells them again to leave her in her pain and loneliness. She says, "No, my daughters, for it is exceedingly bitter for me for your sake that the hand of the LORD has gone out against me" (1:13).

This phrase has to do with how she perceives God's Presence. When the hand of the Lord is on or with someone, they are being blessed. So when she mentions this to the women, she is implying that God has cursed her and turned His back on her, leaving her husband-less, and son-less two times over. Orpah kisses her mother-in-law and says good-bye, but Ruth clings to her.

She tells Ruth to go back home, but Ruth gives the speech that we most often quote from this book.

But Ruth said, "Do not urge me to leave you or to return from following you. For where you go, I will go and where you lodge I will lodge. Your people shall be my people and your God my God. Where you die I will die, and there I will be buried. May the LORD *do so to me and more also if anything but death parts me from you" (1:16—17).*

Naomi looks at this desperate, grieving widow in front of her, holding Ruth's shaking arms in her own, and she knows that Ruth is a woman determined to hitch her wagon to her own. The two of them journey to Israel together—two women with no one to care for them. Two women who have buried the men they love in a land that they're leaving. Two women pressing forward into the unknown, convinced that God has forgotten them.

For some of you, this sense of fear and abandonment and unknown-ness isn't that foreign. You may not have to dig very deeply at all to find the ache. Perhaps you didn't feel Him while your world fell apart, and it's left you not only bruised but mending broken bones. Something deep and hard to express happens when we feel unseen. The light starts to go from your eyes, and you find that over time, emotions just don't run so deep. If nothing can be felt, nothing can hurt.

This is a real, tender place that I have found myself in. It's an honest and haunting kind of pain that sinks an anchor down into dark waters, keeping my little boat out in the middle of a storm with no hope of drifting to the shore. So when I tell you what I'm about to, I want you to know that I have lost vision and sunk deep into grief. I want you to know that just because I eventually caught sight of a lighthouse and was able to make my way back to shore, it doesn't mean that your storm isn't real. But it does mean that it won't storm forever.

If we were friends in real life and there was one moment of this book where I could sit you down and make eye contact to make sure you got a message, this might be it. I would turn off the ringer on my phone and motion for you to sit down across from me, and I'd move aside whatever was between us. No computers or tables or even the jacket you're holding on your lap because you don't plan to stay very long. And once we were there, in that moment, I would look you in the eye and say, "It won't hurt forever."

This is perhaps the hardest part of the gospel to believe at times. How do we trust that the storm is going to end when we're alone out at sea? How do we expect to recover when nothing feels like progress? We come to the end of ourselves in these seasons; the lighthouse, it turns out, can appear as one of a few things. Sometimes, it's the whisper of God that pulls you to Himself. Other times, He gives us the gift of one another. A flesh-and-bone reminder that He still dwells among those He loves and that the Spirit of God is in His people, bringing us back to life so that we can go back into battle and bandage each other's wounds. This is the kindness of community, and without it—without this tremendous grace of God—we would be lost.

For years, I wasn't affirmed in the gifts that I had or the passions that I cared about by the people around me. As a result, I bought into that lie that I had to prove my worth. The conversation was the start of a longer journey of finding freedom, and it had to do a lot with constantly revisiting places of insecurity. In fact, the third night of Camp Well, Jenn and Kelly stood up and wanted to honor someone in the room who was often overlooked. I stood there, camera at the ready, to capture the moment when they announced who that person was. I figured it wasn't in the program, but it'd be clear soon.

And then, in the most unexpected moment of my career as a sidelines person who is just there to do work and nothing else, they motioned toward me. I was in shock. So much so that I put my camera on the table and sat down, overcome and weeping. One by one, these women who were there to cheer on one another stood up with applause to honor my work and I covered my face. Shaking with the overwhelming feeling of being seen, I summoned everything in me to stay there. I wanted to run out or ask them to sit back down. I wasn't sure how to accept that much kindness and appreciation.

It took me back to a moment I had with a counselor back in college. She asked me one day, "Melissa, what are the things that you are good at? Not just for work, but qualities you have that people love?" I was hesitant to give her even one, but she coached me along and wrote them all down. Simple things like, "People say I'm funny," or "I make bread for the girls in my dorm." When it was finished, and I thought I couldn't get any more uncomfortable, she made me sit there while she read the list back to me.

As she did, my general discomfort gave me the same reaction I'd have years later at Camp Well. I burst into tears. She looked at me compassionately and said, "Melissa, it hurts because it's something you've wanted for so long. And it's okay that it's painful to be affirmed." That comment has stuck with me for years because it reminds me that hurt is painful and healing can be painful, too. After years of struggling to be seen, the women at Camp Well were there to remind me that God's grace sometimes looks like friendship and community. It doesn't erase the heartbreak or hardship you've endured, but it certainly offers a safe place to heal.

> God's grace sometimes looks like friendship and community. It doesn't erase the heartbreak or hardship you've endured, but it certainly offers a safe place to heal.

Ruth and Naomi cross the border back into Naomi's hometown—Bethlehem. In Hebrew, *beth* means a place and *lechem* is the word for bread, so the town's name literally means "The Place of Bread." Of course, this isn't just a coincidence that Jesus will be born here—the bread of life. But before that comes to pass, Naomi has left because of a famine, and now she's returning with the hope of finding shelter and food and provision.

As they make their way through the town, there's a stirring. Those who remember her from years before start to talk among themselves with anticipation. Naomi is back. And she's not alone. The curious people ask, "Is this really Naomi?" and instead of a sense of what she'd hoped would be relief, her grief comes back to her. Like being loved again after being left, it's painful. And her response is not shrouded in a fake or forced happiness.

"Do not call me Naomi; call me Mara. For the Almighty has dealt bitterly with me. I went away full, and the Lord has brought me back empty" (1:20–21). The word *mara* is the word for "bitter" in Hebrew. It connotes not only a poor taste but a poor state. Something that tears you apart makes you *mara*. It's a word of grief and ache and the loss of, well, sweetness. When something is consumed that is bitter, it is poisonous. It is, in its purest form, lethal. If you drink bitter water, you die.

Names are important in Scripture because they often have a deeper meaning. Just like when Abram became Abraham, it often marks a new identity. But Naomi's comment is one of renaming her identity after what she perceives will be her fate. I can imagine that after she says those fateful words, "I went away full, and the Lord has brought me back empty," there was a sort of low hum of awkwardness. But I want us to pay attention to this phrase because it's the key sentiment that Naomi is living by. It is her most honest confession and it must be spoken in order for us to know exactly what's happening in her head and her heart.

Now, the next part of the narrative is where most of

us have started the story in the past. We remember Ruth by her connection to the character that enters the scene next: Boaz. Boaz is a man who owns some fields in town that are abundant and overflowing with provision. And he also happens to be a relative of Naomi's, so she knows who he is. At this point, Naomi probably feels a bit responsible for Ruth, whom she has now started calling her daughter (as opposed to her daughter-in-law). This term of affection indicates that Naomi is taking on the role of caregiver to this woman who will not leave her side.

One day, she suggests that Ruth go to the fields to glean. Because they fall into the category of those most vulnerable (widows), they are entitled to take whatever the harvesters missed when they were picking the crops. She goes and picks and Boaz spots her early on. He asks around, and one day, he approaches her and says to her, "Do not go to another field to glean, but stay with us in this one."

Y'all, this is favor from the Lord. Most men in Boaz's position might be annoyed by her, but he knows that she came with Naomi and was caring for her mother-in-law, and so he takes things a step further. When she asks what she's done to be noticed by him, he replies, "All that you have done for your mother-in-law since the death of your husband has been fully told to me, and how you left your father and mother and your native land and came to a people that you did not know before" (2:11).

He blesses her by telling her, "A full reward be given to you by the LORD, the God of Israel, under whose wings you have come to take refuge!" (2:12), and she continues working. At lunchtime, Boaz invites her to his table to be part of his community and afterward tells his workers to stay away from her and not take advantage of her in any way. Boaz recognizes that Ruth is vulnerable, and he chooses to use his influence to protect her. When Ruth goes home, she tells Naomi what has happened, and Naomi feels a sense of relief that there is hope that Ruth may be taken care of. Her focus is her daughter, who not only is finding work that provides for the two of them but might be on the edge of finding an even deeper provision.

Here's the thing about God seeing us individually: It's not just a general sight. No, He sees us and loves us and reveals Himself to us in even the smallest ways. One of the ways that God has specifically spoken to me over the years is in the lives of my dearest friends.

I learned to long for Jesus because I saw other people meet Him. I watched my friend Hannah pour over others in prayer, faithful to see what He sees when she looks at those around her. I watched my friend Jenn recover after a devastating divorce, determined to put her trust in Christ alone. I watched my friend Bre endure loss after loss in her family, fighting to see beauty and adventure, even in the midst of heartbreak. Each time, I saw how specifically and individually He was working in their lives, and it reminded me that He sees all of us that way. He isn't only redeeming Hannah and Jenn and Bre because He only loves them. No, He's redeeming them because it's just what He does as our God and what He intends to do for each and every one of us, even though it might not seem like it's happening at the same time.

The people around us often point out to us the ways that God is at work. We see it when people who know Him deeply walk through struggle and cross over to the other side still breathing. We see it when we hold a baby in our arms that was prayed for. But we also see God's unique Presence in the way He carefully carries us in times of sorrow.

Miraculously, even though it didn't seem possible, we sense God at times when we are the most devastated. We see God's comfort after miscarriages and disappearing heartbeats. We sense His deep love when traumatic memories wake us up from our sleep. We read story after story of how He loves people not just generally but specifically and it can encourage our weary hearts to wait for the Lord. Something deep down isn't letting go, even though we lack the energy and ability to keep our grip.

Of course, waiting for the Lord is far from easy. But over and over again, the people of God are urged to wait. To wait for Him to speak. To wait for Him to move. To wait for Him to come, in His timing, and make all things right. His timing is not our own, but He promises to be with us and that our tears will one day end, even if it's taking more time than we'd like to see that happen.

If we don't understand that God is, in fact, orchestrating things and speaking to us in our own lives, we'll miss out on one of the most important aspects of His character. And if we miss God's movements and acts of redemption in small ways, we might miss that He's got more than our temporary struggles on His mind—He intends to redeem it all.

Naomi, ever the protective and providing mother, tells Ruth to go get really honest with Boaz. A good bit of time has passed now, and so Ruth is no stranger to Boaz and his people. She's a regular at the fields and the threshing floor (the place where crops are prepared for the market or processed for baking/cooking). One night, after having a good meal and a bit of wine, Boaz falls asleep on the threshing floor, making a bed in the heaps of grain. Y'all— he is literally sleeping in the abundance of what used to be famine years before, driving Naomi and her late husband away from their homeland. The Bible is bonkers and beautiful and rich.

Ruth goes to the threshing floor after he's fallen asleep, when no one else is around. She finds him there and does something kind of random to the modern reader. She uncovers his feet. Part of this, one could argue, is to cause him to wake up—cold feet are sure to do the trick. But what comes out of her mouth when he stirs is the really important thing.

He wakes up around midnight and sees her there and has this what-is-happening moment of confusion and he asks, "Who are you?" into the darkness. Ruth replies, "I am Ruth, your servant. Spread your wings over your servant, for you are a redeemer" (3:9).

This phrase about wings has to do with protecting and caring for. It's what Boaz mentioned before when he blessed her in reference to God *under whose wings you take refuge*. This phrase is also sometimes translated as Ruth asking Boaz to cover her with the corner of his robe. Which might seem random until you realize that the Bible is never that random. So you have to understand this piece of Ancient Near Eastern culture. When someone was given a scroll of inheritance or something of great value, it was rolled up and sewn into the hem of their garment. Think of a wallet but more extreme. You wouldn't want to lose it, so you'd literally take it everywhere because of its worth.

This is why Joseph's brothers were mad that their little brother got the coat of many colors from their father—it wasn't just a coat. It was an inheritance and a legacy and monetary provision. This is also why it's powerful and significant that the woman who wouldn't stop bleeding in Luke 8:40–48 was healed by touching the hem of Jesus' robe. His inheritance of healing and hope was given to her in the form of providing healing.

So when Ruth asks for a corner of his robe (or the cover of his wings, as it were), she's really asking for him to take care of her. She's suggesting that he redeem her. And Boaz is a good enough man that he not only agrees, but does things the right way. He knows that there is another man who has the opportunity to redeem her. Back in those days, if a woman's husband died, the honorable thing to do was for his next of male kin to step in and marry her to make sure she was taken care of. Boaz knows that there's another man in town who is a closer relation to her, so he says that he will give that man the chance to do the right thing.

However, if he doesn't step up, Boaz is all in.

"Remain tonight," he says, "and in the morning, if he will redeem you, good; let him do it. But if he is not willing to redeem you, then, as the LORD lives, I will redeem you. Lie down until morning" (3:13).

Ruth goes to sleep, and the next morning before she heads back to Naomi, Boaz rises early and prepares a load of grain. He instructs her to go back to Naomi but makes a request that she bring the grain with her. When she returns, and Naomi asks how it all went, Ruth tells her the details and one sentence stands out: "These six measures of barley he gave to me, for he said to me, 'You must not go back empty-handed to your mother-in-law.'"

This statement pulls us back to months earlier when Naomi told the people, "I went away full, but the LORD has brought me back empty" (1:21). It is no coincidence that these words are so clearly mirrored. The Lord has intended all along to take care of not only Ruth, but Naomi, too. Even though Naomi was convinced that hope is truly lost for her and that her focus will be getting Ruth help because at least then one of them will find hope, God has not forgotten Naomi, and His intentions are being made known.

I am certain there were days and nights when Naomi found herself at a crisis of faith. Not necessarily fearing that God doesn't exist, but for sure thinking that He is not going to uniquely meet her in a specific way. She's in that place of simultaneous faith and doubt. And because she feels like she hasn't been proven wrong, she stays there. All that she sees is famine when the Lord has been providing what she needed along the way: a daughter to mourn with, a companion to travel with, a community to live among. And in that moment when Ruth walks through the door with arms full of barley, Naomi's tired eyes meet Ruth's. She sees the barley and remembers all of the lack—the famine. And she thinks of her boys, buried in the land of Moab near their father. And something in her suddenly *knows* that God has seen her.

And her language of denial and sadness and struggle changes into hope as she advises Ruth to be patient, for "the man will not rest, but will settle the matter today" (3:18).

And he does. The kinsman redeemer responsible to care for Ruth who is with the other men in town is approached by Boaz. And he isn't even given a name. The Hebrew calls him *P'loney Al-Monie*, which translates to "So-and-so" or "What's-his-name." And remember: someone's name often is part of their stories. Saul meets Jesus and becomes "Paul" or "Moses" means "I pulled him out of the water" because it's part of his story. So when we see that the kinsman isn't given a name, it's a way for the narrator to imply that his character was so despicable in not redeeming Ruth that he doesn't deserve a name.

Boaz tells him that Naomi has a field that she is selling which belonged to her late husband. There is very little risk here—it's just land. The man agrees to take on the land. But then, Boaz adds, "When you buy the field from the hand of Naomi, you also buy it from Ruth the Moabite, the widow of the dead, in order to perpetuate the name of the dead in his inheritance" (4:5).

And the redeemer backs out. He is not willing to take on a package deal, let alone one that unites him to a foreign widow. He looks at Boaz and says, "Buy it for yourself" (4:6). This action is wildly disrespectful to Ruth and her late husband. He is refusing to honor the dead and, in doing so, is dishonoring Ruth. It would be as if someone was asked to carry a casket at a funeral and loudly refused because it was too heavy or too hot outside. His true character is revealed as selfish and insulting.

The two men perform the customary actions of passing on the responsibility to Boaz, and he pronounces that all those gathered are witnesses that he will take on the land from Naomi's late husband and he will take Ruth as his wife and they will honor the dead that these women have been grieving over for so long. The community blesses Boaz and wishes him abundance and joy.

Ruth and Boaz get married, and in the last paragraphs of the story, we see the redemption come full circle. Ruth had been married for around ten years when her husband died, and they never had children. In a culture that valued children and didn't have any kind of modern birth control, it was assumed that Ruth had been barren. But we learn that the Lord gives her and Boaz a son. The Bible is full of miraculous birth narratives that mark important moments in the history of God's people. Think of Moses, or Isaac and Jacob, or even Jesus—all were miraculous birth stories. All played a vital role in the story that God has told.

This is what I don't want you to miss: The perspective of God is one in which all of our stories matter. If the lowliest person in a society—an outcast, foreign widow—can be seen and provided for by God, it reveals that this kind of redemption is His way. God sees you, and beyond that, He is working in your life in an individual way. He knows the circumstances of your past, and He is working the details out to remind you of His Presence. Perhaps it's an encouraging note from a friend or a timely word from someone you barely know. Maybe it's the subtle wink of the light coming in your window while you feed your baby that you never thought you'd have, or it's the way someone sees right through your facade and has decided to love you for who you actually are. And sometimes, it can be a combination of those little moments.

> God sees you, and beyond that, He is working in your life in an individual way. He knows the circumstances of your past, and He is working the details out to remind you of His Presence.

A year ago, my friend Jenn got married in what was maybe one of the most redemptive weddings I've ever witnessed. I offered to make a film for Jenn and her fiancé, Rhett, because it's one of the ways I love my people. I was about six weeks away from finishing this book manuscript and feeling absolutely worn, so at the wedding I went to my default mode of staying on the edges of the action, taking photos and video.

During the wedding rehearsal, Jenn and Rhett's friends gave speeches and blessings and told story after story of how God's faithfulness had led to that weekend. At the end, Jenn and Rhett stood up and held hands, and with eyes filled with tears, she said, "I want to thank all of the good men in this room who have loved my friends and given me hope that relationships like that are possible." She saw the faithfulness of God in the lives of others, and it gave her hope after having experienced a devastating loss years before.

As I captured images that night and the following day, I kept my heart distanced from the emotion of it. The morning of the wedding, my dear friend Kelly was sitting at brunch and saw me with my camera and said, "Hey—come sit with us." I declined out of instinct and she said, "You have a seat at this table, Melissa. Come sit here." I felt the tenderness of being a little exposed and pushed it back down.

Later that night at the reception, I saw my friend Andee's mom across the room. I knew she'd been praying over the book-writing process and had been a massive encouragement to me from Northwest Arkansas, but we hadn't really had the chance to talk much in person and the day before had been our first time meeting face to face. I decided I'd talk to her later because she looked busy, and I opted to take a seat and drink some water instead. Suddenly, someone sat down beside me. I looked up to see Andee's sweet mama there with a smile on her face. She put her hand on my arm and said, "You know, we really haven't had the chance to talk." I felt myself come a little more undone at her intentionality and kindness that I couldn't quite express.

As I made my way back to the dance floor, people were telling me to set down my camera and join them and so I finally did. I danced with Jenn and Rhett, our friends from Camp Well, Andee, and all these people who had carried the book with me for so long. It felt like a joyful release after a few wearing months. Exhausted, I went back to the house where I was staying that night and finally drifted off to sleep.

I had a dream about some heartbreak that I'd gone through a month or so before, and it woke me up. It was one of those dreams that resurfaces grief, and when I woke up, it was still so vivid that I had a brief moment of confusion between what was real and what was imagined. Disoriented, I slowly reminded myself that I was in Arkansas; I was single and weary, and in that moment, tears started to come over the weight of it all. And no sooner had I asked Jesus for comfort than I was met with the words of Isaiah 40:31: "Those who hope in the LORD renew their strength" (NIV). Over and over again, I repeated those words and my grief gave way to image after image of the days before: driving on roads we didn't know, toasts that brought life and perspective, a welcoming friend at brunch, a beautiful friend walking down the aisle as her almost-husband wept, kind eye contact with a woman who saw me on the sidelines, dancing with friends from across the country.

This is what it looks like to have that encounter with the living God. These moments of truth and clarity and comfort, no matter how brief, are what it means to be seen by Him. He moves in these and a thousand ways. When God spoke to me in that way, He didn't tell me anything Scripture doesn't already confirm. He never does because His character doesn't change from ancient times until today and into forever. He is always telling His redemptive story in each of our lives, even when it seems that all is lost. And goodness, if that's not good news, I'm not sure what is.

As Naomi holds the miracle baby her friends gather around and say, "Blessed be the LORD, who has not left you this day without a redeemer, and may his name be renowned in Israel! He shall be to you a *restorer of life* and nourisher of your old age, for your daughter-in-law who loves you, who is more to you than seven sons, has given birth to him" (4:14–15).

And as the story in the Book of Ruth ends, "Then Naomi took the child and laid him on her lap and became his nurse. And the women of the neighborhood gave him a name, saying, 'A son has been born to Naomi.' They named him Obed. He was the father of Jesse, the father of David" (4:16–17).

She said that she went away *full*, but He brought her back *empty*. Boaz said, "Don't go back to Naomi *empty*," and the women said, "He shall be to you a *restorer* of life," describing her fullness that she had lost. Her grief was not overlooked, nor was it forgotten. The men who died at the beginning of the story were honored by future generations and their legacy continued to baby Obed, whose bloodline would continue all the way to Christ. If the Lord hadn't restored Naomi in this way, the whole story of Jesus' birth would have changed.

But isn't that just like our God? He never misses a beat; it just might take a moment. But rest assured: If you're still waiting for redemption—it's on its way.

Take heart, dear friend. It's on its way.

CHAPTER SEVEN

Kingdom Mystery

The mystery of God and His Kingdom is something we often feel and seldom recognize. Sometimes, it's a restlessness or a desire to know exactly how the future will play out. Other times, it's grief as we process through a series of events that do not make sense to us. It can also look like a joy of experiencing something so beyond ourselves that we know is a good thing we could never fully feel or we might burst with gratitude. It's felt in a sense of joy and wonder and awe and confusion and hope and overwhelm. And more often than not, the mystery of the Kingdom is something that we forget even exists. Simply put, the mystery of the Kingdom of God is that there are parts of this world and our faith and eternity that we just don't fully grasp.

> Simply put, the mystery of the
> Kingdom of God is that there are
> parts of this world and our faith and
> eternity that we just don't fully grasp.

When I was a kid, I desperately wanted to be a detective. My mother had a tendency to misplace her purse, or her keys, or her wallet, or her address book, so I would look and often find whatever it was that she was missing. We jokingly referred to this as the "Zaldivar Detective Agency." A few months back, I was packing up my childhood room and I came across a little piece of paper with my handwriting on it.

I had carefully written with my best penmanship, "Melissa Zaldivar, Age: 8, Field Agent," in pencil and then laminated the card with Scotch Tape. The other side had three large letters across it: FBI. (I'm certain that I was the youngest ever of the FBI field agents.) The obsession with solving cases went beyond the Zaldivar Detective Agency and fake FBI ID. I would dress up as Sherlock Holmes for Halloween and try to solve mysteries in my neighborhood with my friends. Of course, the biggest mystery we ever really had on our hands was why there was a random tile floor in the vacant lot across the street. The answer was a very obvious one: The house there had burned down years before.

There is something inside me that has wanted answers for as long as I can remember. I was an avid reader and always curious. My number one strength on the StrengthsFinder evaluation is "Learning." From a young age, I was always looking for information. It took me to college and through grad school and into researching for books. It has always been so satisfying to me to have an idea about what I am talking about.

I'm sure that I'm not alone in this because we live in a broader culture that prides itself on awareness and education. People are constantly acting as though they were experts on nearly every subject, offering their two cents in every possible conversation. Something deep in us loves to feel like we know things because it gives us the illusion of authority and control. It leaves no room for questioning or doubt or uncertainty or wonder. Our attempts to solidify our standing often leave us in places where we are working so hard to maintain perceived control that we lose sight of who is really in charge.

A few years ago, I hit a wall and realized that sometimes we don't get answers. We just come out with more questions. And what's a detective to do with that kind of outcome? What does it mean to have faith but to carry doubts? And how does our faith survive the heartbreak and grief of losing a sense of control and safety?

I was in college and had been part of the improv team and we decided to go on a spring retreat. We were a rowdy group of seven to eleven students, depending on the season, and we would have shows every month. We did half improv comedy (think: *Whose Line Is it Anyway?*) and half sketch comedy (think: *Saturday Night Live*). It was the closest group of friends that I had in college, and I don't think I've ever laughed with friends as much as I did with them. While it was mostly fun and games and comedy writing, making fun of the idiosyncrasies of Bible college students in the urban Midwest, we were supposed to also build community with one another. So we decided to do what any other Chicagoan students would: We were going to take a retreat to the suburbs.

I called shotgun, and we climbed into the van we had rented. We pulled onto the freeway via the Ontario Street entrance and were quickly approaching a fork in the road. You could go straight, which would take you west into the suburbs, which was where we wanted to go, or you could go to the right, which would take you to the east suburbs and Indiana.

As we started to accelerate to highway speeds, I was playing the part of navigator and looking down at a map when someone from the backseat shouted the name of the driver. Ahead of us were brake lights. They were red and bright against the gray sky. They were alarming and somehow familiar. As our driver hit the brakes to slow down, I had that moment of knowing that we'd just avoided an accident, and a little wave of relief came over me. But it was immediately overwhelmed by a greater wave of fear, because the car in front of us hadn't just *slowed down*, it had stopped. And all of our driver's efforts to brake were not enough.

Our van had managed to slow to about forty-five leisurely miles per hour before it slammed into the back of the Jeep in front of us. We'd become the fifth car in a six-car pileup on the freeway. I remember looking out my window to the right because I knew that I was about to be in an accident and didn't want to see it happen. Everything in the car went totally silent right before impact. You'd think that it would have been a chaotic moment with people shouting, but I think we all knew that there was nothing we could have done.

After that horrible silence was the sound of glass shattering and metal twisting as the back bumper of that Jeep in front of us crunched into the front end of our van, and when I opened my eyes, I could see the taillights about three feet from my face. Exhaust and dust coming in through the shattered windshield, we sat in silence, probably in shock that we'd really been in an accident. I remember running my hands over my arms and legs and face, making sure nothing was broken or lacerated and finally saying to the other people in the car, "We have to get out of the car—but don't get out on the passenger side because there might be traffic."

I was simultaneously afraid and calm, and until someone asked if people were okay, I didn't want to look around to see for myself, lest I be met with something terrible. We stumbled out of the car and I remember looking up at the city skyline surrounding us, trying to get everything in order. We called our parents and answered questions from the police and got the car towed to an accident investigation site nearby. I absentmindedly licked my lips because they felt dry and was met with the bitterness of airbag dust that had settled on my face. I spit it out and wiped off my nose and cheeks, still in shock and still numb. The tow truck driver's name was Mike Jordan, which seemed strangely fitting for Chicago.

We made it back to campus and I remember walking down the hallway of my dorm with bags in hand, trying to ignore the fact that all I could see in my head was our car careening toward the back of that Jeep. Over and over again, like a film on repeat, I could see it. I tried to be fine but didn't realize that something deep in me had cracked.

See, for weeks, I'd been wrestling with pain around me. People dying, friends experiencing tragedy, and now this accident highlighted to me the reality that not only was the world around me broken, but my own world was fragile, and my own life was fleeting. I started to struggle for the first time with panic attacks and found myself otherwise numb to things going on around me. I remember the first time I was in a car after the accident, we got caught in rush hour and the slow-moving freeway was a sea of brake lights. I stared at my feet and tried not to think about how it felt like everything was too much.

I was convinced that, as a Bible college student, I couldn't let go of my relentless faith in Jesus. And I believed that if I just kept reading my Bible and going to classes, I would feel the way that I'd always felt about Jesus: like things were sweet and He was kind and reliable. But what I found was that for the first time I didn't quite trust that He had good things in mind for me. I didn't doubt His existence or that He was good on the whole, but I *did* believe that He wasn't good to me personally.

When you grow up in a faith community or spend a lot of time in the church, things start to become sort of comfortable and humdrum, and your faith stops being challenged. This is part of the normal cycle of the believer, but it's not a place we can stay forever. There are times in our lives when we push past comfort for the sake of cultivating something deeper because the alternative is stagnancy and numbness and we can stop engaging altogether. Our faith is not always exciting and that's okay. This doesn't mean that we have to pretend things are fine when they aren't, but it does mean we have to hold the tension of being broken and hoping for restoration, even if it's not coming for a while.

As the days after the accident turned to weeks and months, I found myself with the strange habit of sleeping next to my Bible. Part of that came from a knowledge that God hadn't changed even though I was struggling with anxiety and doubt. The other part of me was honest enough to know that whenever I opened my Bible, I didn't know where to begin. Like putting your feet in before you jump into the pool, I needed to feel like I was close to being in before I could totally commit again. I would lie on my side with my Bible beside me, a familiar but faraway presence in a time of grief.

I knew that it was full of truth, but I wasn't sure if I was ready to explore that truth in the same ways I did before the breaking down happened. In retrospect, I was having a crisis of faith of sorts. Not so much that God wasn't real, but that He was nothing like I'd assumed for all these years. That He was distant and concerned with other matters, leaving me behind, looking away and removing a kind gaze that had been my safety for so long.

I remember the day that I started taking little steps toward a new sort of season of faith—one that wasn't as naïve or ignorant. I started praying by reciting the Apostles' Creed. I'd been in a class about systematic theology and we'd get extra credit if we memorized the creed, so I'd committed it to memory and it felt like an okay place to start rebuilding what had been forgotten.

The Apostles' Creed dates back thousands of years and is a quick, straightforward statement of faith that Christians have lived by for centuries. The Bible is long, so this concise series of statements was a way for Christians to say, "This is what I believe," and also know what the biggest deals are in the Christian faith. For example, some people argue about what we call "minor" issues. Things like how to baptize or how often you should receive communion. While those are important topics, their exact details and practice vary so you can be gracious, and if someone holds a different opinion, you don't get to assume they're a heretic.

I grew up in the Baptist tradition and we celebrated communion once a month. But now, I go to a church that celebrates it every week. And both have their reasons, but no one is going to be considered "un-Christian" for their practice in this case. However, if a church decided to go against the major tenets of the faith, there would be a problem. If they decided that Jesus wasn't really divine or that God didn't really create the heavens and the earth, it would be a much bigger deal.

I knew that some of the nuances of my faith were shifting, but I also knew that the major parts of my faith were still intact. So I would recite the Creed to myself just to remember that there was solid ground to stand on. Ground that is based on the words of Scripture and that generation after generation has found to be true. A book by someone like C. S. Lewis or another well-known Christian is helpful, but it isn't considered church tradition, simply because it's not so widely agreed upon and tested over the course of time. The Creeds were written to remind us that we're not alone, and they are based on the Word of God.

As I slowly rebuilt the muscles of my faith and ventured back into reading Scripture and asking questions I hadn't asked before, I found that I was met with the kindness of Jesus. Our relationship started to feel much more like a partnership because I saw the ways that He carried me at a pace I could handle. I remember a professor playing this song about marriage being hard and for some reason it resonated so deeply with me that I couldn't stop listening to it.

Part of the mystery of the Kingdom of God is the fact that He continues to work out our faith by His grace. Even when we're in a season of grief or loneliness. Even when we're not sure that His love is big enough to cover our shortcomings. Even when we're reading the Bible daily, constantly feeling renewed. Our salvation is something that we have and that we continually are given. We are being saved daily, hourly, moment by moment, and breath by breath. This work of sanctification—the process of being made holy—is something that will continue on in every season until one day we're face to face with Jesus.

* * *

In 1 Corinthians 13, the famed love chapter, Paul is talking about love and how everything shifts and changes and fades away, but the three things that remain are faith, hope, and love. He writes about how when Jesus returns, everything will come clearly into focus, and in verses 11–12, he says, "When I was a child, I spoke like a child, I thought like a child, I reasoned like a child. When I became a man, I gave up childish ways. For now we see in a mirror dimly, but then face to face. Now I know in part; then I shall know fully, even as I have been fully known."

This beautiful image of how we grow into who we're becoming is a great reminder of the forward motion and progression of our faith. In some mysterious way, we can see who God is, but it's not the fullest understanding right now. Corinth, the community that this letter was intended for, was a place where mirror and glass making was part of the local business community. And so they would have understood the idea of reflection in a unique way.

If a mirror is dim, you can make out something in the reflection, but it won't be very clear. And it certainly isn't the same as looking at someone face to face.

My friend Andee and I were discussing this and she remarked, "In a reflection, you aren't seeing the actual person, let alone who they are and what is inside of them." The amount of clarity we have around our faith at times is a dim mirror at best when compared to the clarity we will one day have when we see the fullness of the Kingdom. But for now? We have a tension to hold.

••

> The amount of clarity we have around our faith at times is a dim mirror at best when compared to the clarity we will one day have when we see the fullness of the Kingdom.

••

In that season of wanting answers, I found that there is a beautiful tension in this life in which we cling both to the major tenets of the faith and also to the fact that there is mystery in what we believe. I never got an exact answer as to why we crashed. I never got a concrete reply as to why we didn't die. There was an unknown-ness to things, but still a strong sense of knowing God. And this is what built my faith back up. It was the fact that God was not just a set of doctrines to read and memorize, but He was all those statements of the Creed and so much more in reality and practice.

There are two perspectives at play in our faith at all times: the human and the divine. We can experience only our own human perspective. We can come into contact with the divine through the person of Jesus Christ, but we will not know His perspective or reasoning or

145

experience on this side of eternity. This is something that our culture really has a hard time with because we live in a day and age where we expect that everything can be known and nothing has to be a mystery. But when we follow that trail, it always comes up to a dead end. We can understand only so much, and luckily, we don't have to put all of our hope into ourselves.

I remember a professor once explaining that the things of God are often a mystery to us. For example, God is triune, meaning He is three persons in one. The Father, the Son, and the Holy Spirit are all distinct persons, but are also completely unified. This is, in a word, a mystery. A smart-aleck student raised his hand and said, "Isn't the point of a mystery to solve it?"

The professor paused, smiled, and said, "If you're Nancy Drew."

See, there are mysteries that we solve and there are things that are mysterious and we will never fully grasp from our human perspectives. But that doesn't mean we shouldn't ask about them or try to understand them. We often assume that if we don't know the answer, we should just avoid asking questions. That if something can't be fully understood, we should stay away. We assume that the mystery and the I-don't-know-ness of the Kingdom of God indicate a lack of clarity and therefore a lack of information. But in reality, the opposite is true—because mysteries are complex, that means we can ask and ask and wonder and we'll never get to the bottom. We can never dig all the way into how much God loves His people.

We can never touch the floor of His grace. We can never fathom the ways of the divine.

One year, I met weekly with my friend Joelinda for prayer. We were in a season of lots of transition and uncertainty finishing out our time in seminary. I realized that our faith felt a lot like, "I don't know—but I know." There was confidence in the character of God, but there was a lot of questioning about where we were going and who we were becoming. I wrote it down on a canvas for both of us, and it became our motto. To walk into that mystery and to walk it out together was a gift. To have someone else who was a little scared but still certain in Jesus tethered me to my faith and the mystery of how it was being worked out in some powerful way.

There is always a tension here that we have to carry out. We have to recognize our humanity and our desire to know ALL THE THINGS, but also trust that a sovereign God is ruling over the Kingdom that lasts forever. That His eternal Kingdom is in contrast to our earthly one that's always changing and failing and breaking and in process.

What unites us all in human experience is sometimes the unknown-ness of the Kingdom. It's the fact that none of us can control or predict the future. And the key to living in the mystery of what we do not know is connecting with the God who can be eternally known, because He is vast and deep and infinite. In fact, God is far beyond our comprehension and that is what makes Him who He is. He is, in a word, *holy*.

....

And the key to living in the mystery
of what we do not know is
connecting with the God who can be
eternally known, because He is vast
and deep and infinite.

....

Holiness has to do with something that is set apart. It is not of this world and sacred. Often used to refer to temple practices or God Himself, this word has an "otherness" feel to it. Something that is holy is not man-made. It is consecrated and unique and of eternal value. Think of royal temple courts or sanctuaries or heaven itself. God's people are called "holy" because of their association and relationship with a holy God. There are holy holidays, holy practices, and holy places, and the thread that connects them all together is the holiness of the God that they are oriented toward.

We as God's people are set apart, a holy community, to do God's work and build His Kingdom. We're not here to have every answer or to solve every problem, but we are here to be His and to focus on what He is doing and to glorify Him. Everything about our lives ought to be ordered to ultimately be pointed toward Him. Our relationships, our jobs, our desires—all of these can be aimed at God. Because if they aren't? We're aiming at ourselves again, and we're going to fizzle out and fall short and doubt and lose our faith because it isn't built on what actually matters.

This contrast between our own ways and God's holiness allows us to see that there are things we cannot see and concepts that we cannot master and an immediate future we cannot predict, but it also gives us security in that we're able to trust all those things to a God whose character we can know and whose kindness we can lean into and whose sovereignty we can rely on. For every mystery that we cannot fully comprehend, He knows every piece of the puzzle. We can know only a fraction of a percent of the way that world works and the vastness of the Kingdom of God, but He knows every single percentage without even trying.

We often fear the not-knowing because it feels a lot like being blindfolded. When we find ourselves at a crossroads between where we stand and where we could possibly go, we ask God for clarity. Over and over again, we believe that if God will just tell us what's going to happen, we will be fine. But that's not supposed to be the end goal of our faith, or all we want in a God we are willing to trust is answers like some kind of genie who exists only to give us our three wishes.

Imagine you met someone that you were ready to spend your whole life with. And over time, you knew enough to know them as someone with reliable character and were certain they could be trusted. But then, when it came time for the vows, you stipulated that you'd be with them only if every argument went your way and every choice was yours only and they had to guarantee that you'd never move or change jobs or that you'd have a specific number of children. That would be ridiculous, right?

So why is it that we do this to God? Why do we demand that the world revolve around us and ask Him over and over to just tell us what is going to happen? Or if we don't like where He is leading us, we act as though His kindness and grace have not been enough. We become frustrated by the unanswered questions and demand clarity.

I can't tell you the number of times I've heard the prayer request of "clarity." In his book *Ruthless Trust*, Brennan Manning writes:

When the brilliant ethicist John Kavanaugh went to work for three months at "the house of the dying" in Calcutta, he was seeking a clear answer as to how best to spend the rest of his life. On the first morning there he met Mother Teresa. She asked, "And what can I do for you?" Kavanaugh asked her to pray for him.

"What do you want me to pray for?" she asked. He voiced the request that he had borne thousands of miles from the United States. "Pray that I have clarity."

She said firmly, "No, I will not do that." When he asked her why, she said, "Clarity is the last thing you are clinging to and must let go of." When Kavanaugh commented that she always seemed to have the clarity he longed for, she laughed and said, "I have never had clarity; what I have always had is trust. So I will pray that you will trust God."

This perhaps is the most challenging part of the way that the Kingdom of God is a mystery: We have to trust that it's not a mystery to God. We have to remember that because He is a set-apart, holy, other sort of God, things are not a mere dim reflection to Him. Rather, He looks straight at us and fully knows us. He not only sees our outward appearance but knows our inward appearance as well, and the main point isn't the mystery of the things we encounter, it's the fact that God is in control of all of it.

As I went through that season of doubt after the car accident, I found that what steadied me wasn't the Creed; it was the character of God that the Creed was reminding me of. It was the fact that the God we know is so vast that we'll never come to the end of knowing Him. And that the more I read Scripture and learn about who He is, the more I can trust that He knows what He's doing. He is a God whose Presence is our good. He's a God who, in a time where patriarchy was the law of the land, spoke to and elevated the dignity of women. He's a God who gives Israel chance after chance to follow Him, even though they constantly lose hope and faith and vision. He is the God who looks mystery in the face and is not fazed because it all makes perfect sense to Him.

The Kingdom of God is a mystery to us because it

doesn't always make sense to us, but we can trust that we're going in the right direction when we follow a God who knows all of it. The detective in me wants to get to the bottom of things, but I have learned that the real quest isn't about knowing everything or being an expert or predicting what's next, but it's about focusing my eyes on God Himself.

We do not know, but we know. We may not see the purpose behind everything, but we can trust that God has an end in mind that redeems all of it. We look into a mirror dimly—at best—but can take comfort in the fact that His vision is clear and His love is for us and His aim is redemption. Come what may, in every mysterious season of our faith, we can trust that He will not waver and He does not fail.

CHAPTER EIGHT

Just Do the Dang Thing

The first time we meet Peter in Luke 5, he's been out fishing all night, out to sea for hours on end with nothing to show for it. He was absolutely exhausted, ready to crash, but still having so much to do before he can go home. The Sea of Galilee isn't very big and sits in the middle of Israel just north of the Dead Sea. It feels like more of a massive lake, but nevertheless was the livelihood of fishing communities of the Ancient Near East.

As Peter and his friends bring in their two boats and make their way back to the shore to start finishing out their night, there's a large crowd in the distance. They've been following a new preacher named Jesus as He speaks and He's gotten to a place where He needs to amplify His voice a bit more. The solution? Preach from a boat.

With tired eyes and yawny temperaments, the defeated fishermen start the cleaning process. The nets are likely covered with algae and whatever else might have been in the water and so they have to clean them in order to prepare them for the next attempt at a catch. And as they stand there, frustrated and ready to be done, Jesus approaches. They know who He is—everyone does. A Rabbi who has been making claims about good news and healing people who have been broken their entire lives. Word gets around about a person like that.

As the crowds move closer to the shoreline, He steps onto the dock and makes eye contact with Peter. He asks if Peter can take the boat back out again. Something in Peter is probably annoyed. Something in Peter probably makes excuses. But something else compels him to lift the nets back into the boat and push out to sea. I wonder if it was a catch in his chest or just an inkling that moved the needle from a *no* to a *yes*, but he steps to the side, welcoming Jesus into his boat.

This thing that Peter does here is strange and risky in a small, small way. Jesus is asking for a few hours of his time, nothing more. Peter believes that while this isn't convenient, it'll likely be the last time he encounters this man, so he obliges. He has no idea what he's in for. This risk seems isolated, but nothing could be further from the truth.

A few months ago, I was coming back from a trip overseas and I found myself stuck in the middle of the customs line at the airport. I started making small talk with a man who had come from Wales, where he'd been visiting his girlfriend. We discussed relationships and the UK, and as we inched toward the front of the line to complete the final stage of getting back into the country, I asked him what he did for a living. "Oh, I'm a fisherman," he said.

I thought of Peter and smiled as I said, "So if you had been fishing all night and caught absolutely nothing and then someone said, 'Let's go back out,' what would your reply be?" At that moment, a TSA agent waved for me to come forward. I stepped toward the agent's desk, but did so walking backward so that I could hear this man's reply: "Man, I'd tell them my auntie was sick or something. I'd make up any excuse to not go back out."

Much of the hope of Scripture is pointing us forward. At the start, when He built that beautiful Kingdom and everything broke, God started moving things back together. He reminded Adam and Eve that the broken mess that sin had made wasn't forever but one day everything would be okay again. He promised that Jesus would come for them. Jesus promised the Holy Spirit to be our guide until His return. It's the overarching narrative of Scripture that the people of God are always moving toward nearness with God. Even on our darkest days, we can rest in the comfort that He is coming, and He is moving, and who we are now is not who we will be.

....

Even on our darkest days, we can
rest in the comfort that He is
coming, and He is moving, and who
we are now is not who we will be.

....

So when we step out of our comfort zone, in faith, toward something we know the Lord has put into our hearts, we can trust that He has every intention of walking with us through it. We aren't just making moves apart from Him. In fact, if He is ever-present, then we are never taking leaps of faith into the unknown—because He is the one who knows exactly what is going to happen.

Peter doesn't have that information quite yet. What he knows is that this man is going to preach from the boat and then they'll be home free. As Jesus finishes His sermon to the masses, He steps back into the center of the boat while Peter stands at the helm, and Jesus says with a twinkle in his eye, "Put out into the deep and let down your nets for a catch."

They must think He is insane. The nets are clean, the men are sleep deprived from a night out on the water, and Peter finally speaks some logic into the situation.

"Here's the thing. We worked all night, and nothing happened." Jesus and Peter look at each other in silence and Peter continues, "But at your word, I will let down the nets."

On some level, Peter knows that there is a thing bigger than himself at play here. And every inner voice that has been asking him not to take a risk is suddenly drowned out by an invitation from Jesus to let down the dang nets.

I'm certain there was tired muttering and the feeling of inconvenience being given off from the others, but Peter agreed to make the trip, so they went along with it. A few stayed back—no need for two ships during a fishing outing guaranteed to be a bust.

As Peter and his crew let down the nets, they watch the

ropes fade deeper and deeper into the water, swaying back and forth with the ebb of the sea, floating on the top for a moment before taking on water that weighs them down and out of sight, into the murky depths.

Silence. A tense sigh of resignation from one of the men because the clean net is going to have to be rewashed and now the sun is higher, which means exhausting and hot work. The boat rocks back and forth gently and Peter's avoiding the glares of his friends.

Suddenly, there's a different sort of creak and the ropes begin to pull tighter and tighter. A shocked Peter rushes to the side of the boat and looks down to see that the nets are filling with thousands of fish. Right where there had been nothing all night, there is suddenly abundance in the day. His excitement turns to concern as they try to reel the fish in but are realizing that there are simply too many fish. The one boat can't handle them all.

He rushes to the opposite side of the boat, closer to the shore. His other friends are standing on the dock by their boat, a hand up to block the morning sun, squinting at the commotion offshore. Peter is waving his hands and can't get the words out, but the others know what to do. They trip over themselves, ready their vessel, and sail out to join Peter and his crew, taking on more of the abundance so they can haul it all in.

It's pandemonium. Joy and confusion and disbelief overtake them. The change in plans was not a waste. The fish came in and provided for these career fishermen. It's. A. Miracle. (See Luke 5:1–11.)

* * *

My last year of seminary was a roller coaster ride, and if I can be honest, I really hate roller coasters. I went on Space Mountain at Disneyland when I was a kid, but I was a little too small and kept bumping my head on the seat and came out with a terrible headache. You might think that I'm the kind of person who loves the thrill of a roller coaster, but I'm actually a pretty anxious, calculated person who keeps finding herself in situations just outside her comfort zone. Sometimes it's an exciting thing to have a lot of adventure in your life, but if I'm honest, I crave the slow, steady pace of earlier seasons in my life.

It was the fall of 2014, and I had one semester left in my master's program studying theology. Four classes and I was home free, or so I thought. A few challenging and hard things happened that I needed to process and grieve about, but I had agreed to photograph a wedding in Germany the following week. So I kept pushing past my grief, hoping that I could outrun it. Turns out, you really can't. My friend Jess was studying in Europe, so she met me at the Frankfurt Airport, and by the time we got to the apartment we were staying at, I was barely holding things together.

Night fell, and I sat there in a full-on panic, trying to get my grip back, but all I could do was tighten every muscle in my body. I was determined to keep control. A year before, my counselor had casually mentioned anxiety medication and so I had gotten a prescription for antianxiety pills, which I had with me, but I didn't want to bring myself to actually take one for some reason. There I sat, in the dark, white-knuckle grip on the bottle, unwilling to find relief. I fought and fought my panic for days, all the while photographing a wedding and exploring Heidelberg Castle and slowly, my anxiety started to leave, but I still felt haunted by that moment. Haunted by the look on sweet Jess's face as she helplessly held my hand. Haunted by the fact that I was too full of pride to admit how bad my anxiety was and to just swallow the pill. Haunted by the reality that things were not, in fact, in my control.

I came home, dropped two classes, and decided to take it slow and steady in the last year of seminary, extending my time by a semester. For the first time in years, I could be slow and intentional and go to counseling and focus on my soul. This, of course, was what seminary used to be back in the day. A season of contemplation, slowness, and discipline. These days, it's easy to turn it into a rigorous academic experience, and by the time graduates go into full-time ministry, they're halfway to burnout.

It's easy to ignore the feelings that we're experiencing and the yellow flags that turn orange and then red. It's easy not to address our emotional and mental states, but they are part of who we are. We believe that the aim of our faith is to just be fine, but fine does not equal healthy. A healthy person feels their feelings in deep and true and good ways, not bottling things up but facing them, finding their roots, and addressing them well.

Our human-ness is what Christ fully experienced and He came to cover all of our shortcomings and struggles and broken pieces. My friend Cassie says it like this: "Because of what Christ has done, we have nothing to lose and nothing to gain." We simply come as we are, and no amount of earning is going to get us closer to God than Jesus brings us because of the cross.

We ignore the brokenness and push forward into the achievement as if we do have something to lose or gain. But in light of the Presence of God, we really have nothing else to prove. No amount of work will make me better than my neighbors. No amount of wit will make me more important than the woman next to me at the grocery store. No words will ever give me more worth than a child who cannot even speak yet. All of our effort to appear perfect is wasted. All of our attempts to do things with excellence come up short. And we are guilty of doing this not only to ourselves, but to others as well—especially those in Scripture.

How do we remember Judas? We remember that he betrayed Jesus. We forget that he hated himself for it and repented before the chief priests and was so remorseful he ended his own life after trying to give back the blood money he'd sold Jesus for.

How do we remember Eve? We remember that she sinned, and it ruined everything. As if we would have done something so differently. We forget that she knew God face to face and was created for community. We forget that she lost her son at the murderous hands of her firstborn. We forget that she experienced the pain of childbirth with no one to truly walk her through what to expect. We have no pity for the mother of all the living.

And Peter? We just remember the darkness of his denials. We remember how he chickened out and couldn't be faithful to Jesus. We read his story of saying it three times and we scoff at how we would be so much more faithful. We forget that man standing and looking over the edge of the boat as the nets start to break from the force of thousands of miracles pulling at the ropes.

Hindsight is 20/20 and we often judge these individuals for their lack of faith and action, but when it comes to our own lives, there's hardly ever a moment when we would respond in a different way. The people of God, it turns out, never see what's coming next. Shocker. If the Lord asked me to go discuss emancipation with Pharaoh? I'd probably go take a nap. If He asked me to consider leading a nation, I would be out. Heck, if He asked me to stop watching *The West Wing*, I'd hesitate. If we refuse to have grace for those in the Bible, we have forgotten that we are no different than they are. We believe that we would never sin or betray or sell our Savior, but the reality is, we might even do it for much less.

We are hesitant to put our reputations on the line because it involves risk. And the fact of the matter is that risk is hard because we're handing over the reins to someone else. It's a risk to let your child take the wheel for the first time when they're learning to drive. It's a risk when you tell someone that you love them because you don't know

161

what their response may be. It's a risk to go out on a limb in any way because it's an admission that you cannot be the one in charge of the outcome. And in that way? We are called to be a people always ready to take risks.

But if I can be honest, I really don't think it's just the risk we are afraid of. The real fear is that on the other side we'll be met with pain or failure or disapproval. We're not willing to jump off proverbial cliffs because we assume that the parachute won't open and we'll break our legs on landing.

The good news here is this: We are met, always, by a God who is consistent and entirely in control and entirely forgiving when we inevitably mess things up. He wouldn't need to be a God of redemption if nothing needed to be redeemed.

....

We are met, always, by a God who is consistent and entirely in control and entirely forgiving when we inevitably mess things up. He wouldn't need to be a God of redemption if nothing needed to be redeemed.

....

As Peter stands on the boat, everyone laughs and holds their forehead in disbelief as they prepare the haul for processing. The boats are sinking lower into the water because of the sheer weight of the fish. In the midst of the cheers and the shock, he looks over to Jesus, who smiles like someone watching their child open a surprise gift. Peter makes eye contact and his head kind of turns a bit as if to say, "You knew the whole time, didn't you?" He walks to Jesus and falls down at his feet, grateful and relieved and overcome.

"Depart from me, for I am a sinful man, O Lord," Peter says in Luke 5:8. He knows now that he is in the presence of a mighty and benevolent and perfect miracle worker. And Peter knows the doubt and the cynicism and the brokenness that he himself carries daily. But so does Jesus. And Jesus replies, "Do not be afraid; from now on you will be catching men" (5:10).

I want to stop for a moment and zoom in on that first phrase: "Do not be afraid." We tend to read that as if Jesus were asking Peter to stop feeling his feelings and we often take phrases like that and use them to argue the point that, as Christians we're not allowed to be afraid or overwhelmed or scared.

The Greek word here is *phobos*, which is where we get our word "phobia." And there are a few ways it's used. Sometimes it's over-reverence or awe. Other times it's seen when someone is in a situation that is terrible or scary. But the phrase "Do not fear" is often used in response to someone who is clearly upset because they've come into contact with something holy. This admonishment not to fear is found, for example, surrounding miracles or in miracle narratives.

We see this phrase in this context when Jairus' daughter dies in Mark 5. Jairus is looking for Jesus to heal his sick daughter, and while he's imploring Jesus to come to her, someone shows up and tells them that she has died. They say, "Your daughter is dead. Why trouble the Teacher any further?" (v. 35).

Jesus looks at Jairus and says, "Do not be afraid, only believe" (v. 36 NKJV). He takes only Peter and James and John with Him, and when they get to the girl's house, He tells them that the child is only sleeping. The mourners scoff at Him because she is clearly dead. But Jesus speaks to her and she comes back to life. A miracle happens; the child is alive.

When Mary, the mother of Jesus, is greeted by an angel in Luke 1, the divine being starts talking to her, saying, "Greetings, O favored one, the Lord is with you!" (v. 28). Mary starts to freak out a little bit and the next words out of the angel's mouth? "Do not be afraid, Mary" (v. 30). This same phrase comforts her because the angel recognizes the same thing Jesus does: We mere humans cannot deal when it comes to encountering the power of the living God.

When Jesus is on the mount of transfiguration in Matthew 17, He again takes Peter, James, and John with Him and they witness for a brief moment His holiness. His face "shone like the sun, and His clothes became white as light. And behold, there appeared Moses and Elijah, talking with him" (vv. 2–3).

Now this next part makes me laugh, to be honest. Peter just *has* to get a word in. "And Peter said to Jesus, 'Lord, it is good that we are here. If you wish, I will make three tents here, one for you and one for Moses and one for Elijah" (v. 4).

Classic Peter has seen some crazy things and is trying to convince Jesus that he's the chillest, most casual person who ever walked the earth. It's as if he's trying to be so cool that you can almost see it immediately going wrong. "Hey, Jesus. I think all of this is super fine and I'm not freaking out at all that You're basically light itself, and Moses and Elijah, two of the greatest leaders of all in the history of our people, have showed up at this thing posthumously. Not a big deal *at all.*"

Next verse: "He was still speaking when behold, a bright cloud overshadowed them, and a voice from the cloud said, 'This is my beloved son, with whom I am well pleased; listen to him.' When the disciples heard this, they fell to their faces and were terrified" (vv. 5–6). *While Peter is speaking, God has to proclaim what is happening in order to get Peter to drop the act.* He comes off his high horse pretty solidly and is back on the ground, fully terrified because this situation is bananas and his facade is not cutting it.

And what does Jesus do? He walks over, and the Scripture says, "Jesus came and touched them and said, 'Arise, and do not be afraid.' When they lifted up their eyes, they saw no one but Jesus only" (vv. 7–8 NKJV). The word there, "touch," is used when Jesus touches someone to heal them, but it goes beyond a physical action. It is a touch that goes right to someone's soul to bring healing to them completely. Jesus didn't just give them a quick pat on the back. No, he steadied them to their very core.

This Greek phrase, a command not to be fearful during a miraculous event, occurs at other moments, too. It shows up when Jesus walks on water toward the disciples on a boat in the middle of the night, and they shout, "It is a ghost!" And he says, "Take heart; it is I. Do not be afraid" (Matthew 14:26–27). And it also appears when the tomb is empty and the followers of Jesus believe his body has been stolen. An angel appears and says, "Do not be afraid, for I know that you seek Jesus who was crucified" (Matthew 28:5 NKJV).

Each time this phrase is used, there's always a follow-up of good news or reassurance.

Don't be afraid that your daughter has died—it isn't the end of the story.

Don't be afraid that an angel has appeared—Jesus is coming, and you don't know Him yet but He's going to change everything.

Don't be afraid that the power of God is so strong—stand up.

Don't be afraid that it's a ghost—it's actually your Savior.

Don't be afraid that the tomb is empty, and you think the body was stolen—He is alive.

A commentator in the *Dictionary of New Testament Theology* says it like this: "The fear of men is taken away from them by security in God." This is the power of "do not be afraid." He isn't suggesting that they stop feeling an emotion; He's assuring them that something else is going on. He is recognizing the humanity in each of these people and steadying them with His words. He knows that their fear is due to the fact that they're coming to the natural conclusion, but there is something *supernatural* going on. Each time this phrase is used, it is someone with spiritual authority speaking to humans and letting them know that *it's not what you think.*

So when Jesus tells Peter on the boat, "Do not be afraid," He is introducing this simple fisherman to the miraculous and letting him know that the conclusion is not one that you'd expect. He's revealing to Peter the reality that when God calls you to take a risk, He meets you in it. Something miraculous is pointing to something glorious.

The reason we don't risk is because we believe that we know the outcome and it will be the worst-case scenario. We start relationships with, "What if we break up?" and we quit jobs thinking, "What if I don't get another job?" We don't venture into things that aren't comfortable out of a fear that suddenly things will be out of our control. We forget who God is and we start to inch back toward the shore, too afraid to put our boat out on the water.

The Presence of God brings comfort into our fear and lets us step out, even when we're still afraid, into something greater and allows us to take risks because we know that He's on the other side, and not only that, He is walking through it with us, full of power and kindness. Corrie ten Boom famously once said, "Never be afraid to trust an unknown future to a known God."

Peter first catches a glimpse of the kindness of Jesus that day on the boat. And he would continue to see miracles but struggle with his own disbelief. He would always be a skeptic or try to prove himself with his own wit or ability or perceived wisdom.

At one point, in Matthew 16, Jesus asks Peter who Peter thinks Jesus is. And he immediately, enthusiastically, replies, "You are the Christ, the Son of the living God" (v. 16). Jesus commends him for starting to get that what's going on is bigger than him and his own wisdom. Peter seems to have come a long way in his faith journey by our modern-day assumption that to be put together and confident is to be spiritually successful.

Just a few verses later, Jesus reveals that He's going to die but that He will rise again and it'll all be okay. And what does Peter do? "And Peter took him aside and began to rebuke him, saying, 'Far be it from you, Lord! This shall never happen to you'" (v. 22). Peter is rebuking Jesus not ten verses after he swore that Jesus was the Son of the Living God. This is where Jesus famously tells Peter to stop it by saying, "Get behind me, Satan! You are a hindrance to me. For you are not setting your mind on the things of God, but on the things of man" (v. 23).

Peter is still that nervous fisherman looking around at his tired crew, worried that he might be wrong about all of this. Worried that if he doesn't keep up appearances, people might think he's crazy. Peter wants to follow Jesus but gets caught up in a lot of fear that pushes him to doubt that what's going on is something extraordinary.

Two chapters before that rebuking moment, he had been walking on water with Jesus. But what happened? He took his eyes off Jesus and started to sink, crying out, "Save me!" Still, Jesus takes Peter with Him to his most intimate, vulnerable moments. Peter witnesses the full breadth of what Christ revealed to people during His ministry. He saw the fish breaking the nets. He witnessed thousands of people being fed with hardly any food. He was there when Jesus was transfigured. He watched as Jesus walked on the water, His figure moving into focus through the darkness of the night. But he still questions and fears and struggles and denies and tries to prove himself over and over again.

And yet—knowing all of this would happen, Jesus says, "On this rock, I will build my Church and the gates of hell will not prevail against it" (v. 18). Peter is trusted over and over again, and we don't understand why until we realize that Peter is all of us. If God had trusted only perfect men who never struggled with anxiety or doubt in His plan, then we would be right to assume that feeling afraid is wrong and risk is unsafe.

We would be right never to forgive. We would be right never to have mercy. We would be right to think that our faithfulness is about being flawless and un-messy. We would be right to think that grace is for the weak. We would be right to think that risks are a bad idea.

But do not be afraid—it's not what you think.

Risk for the sake of risk is recklessness. Risk for the sake of obedience to what God is asking of us is freedom. And that risk is really no risk at all because the nearness of a faithful, sovereign, in-control God guarantees that we're making the right call in the long run.

So often, we are like Peter, giving a thousand logical reasons for why it's important to have our bases covered. And I am not saying that we're not supposed to be responsible and wise stewards of what we've been given, but I am saying that when we try to use that language to speak against what He is calling us to, we're venturing into dangerous territory. We become more concerned with our own plans than His. We assume that we know more than He does and that's just outright arrogance. Wise decisions require a lot of prayer and listening to what it is that the Lord has to say about things. It may feel easy, or it may be hard.

Sometimes, risk is asking a friend to go get coffee. Sometimes, it's a job change. Sometimes, it's a cross-country move or choosing a school for your child. But always, always, the risks we take will be worth it on the other side if they're seen through the lens of the Presence of God. I'm sure that's not wildly comforting for those of you who are in the middle of or at the start of a risky move. When we're taking the leap, we are almost always terrified out of our minds.

I remember one summer day a few years ago I visited the grave of D. L. Moody. He was an evangelist a few centuries ago and led revivals around the globe. He was like the Billy Graham of the 1800s. I'd been reading his biography and some of his sermons and gathered that he was a pretty no-nonsense guy who just said things like they were.

There I stood in western Massachusetts, alone in front of his headstone, and I finally just said all the things I was thinking about my future. I pretended to have a conversation with this giant of the faith and blurted out, "D.L., you led great revivals and saw so many incredible things and I know that you're not here, but I'm facing the start of ministry and it feels like nothing is stable and everything is shaky and I'm afraid I'll ruin things or not be good enough or fail and I just need to say out loud that I'm terrified."

As I spoke this confession to the air in front of us, I imagined what D. L. Moody would say to me if he were there. When you're a historian, you get to know people from the past really well and could imagine pretty clearly what they would think about almost anything. In that moment, I imagined that D. L. Moody would probably do two things: He'd laugh a deep, belly laugh, and he'd say, "Well, what did you expect?"

Here's the thing about risk: We pretend that we like it and that we're brave about it, but the fact of the matter is that we're really only into it if it's a calculated risk. An actual risk is not very glamorous, and there's a decent chance you'll wonder where you left your brain in the pursuit of *literally God knows what.*

When Jesus tells Peter in Matthew 26 that he's going to deny Him three times, Peter is in disbelief. He swears his loyalty. But a few hours later, he finds himself face to face with people who ask, "Aren't you one of his disciples?" And three times, Peter says "I am not!" Meanwhile, a few paragraphs earlier, Jesus is on trial and three times they ask, "Are you really the Christ as you say you are?" and three times, he says, "Yes. I am."

These two passages are meant to mirror each other to show the image of man and the image of a faithful Messiah. To show that where Peter backs out, Jesus presses in. And three days later, when Christ rises from the dead, He goes back to that sea where Peter first took Him out on the water.

Peter, distraught and discouraged, has gone back to the life he knew before: He goes fishing. And as he comes back to the shore, he sees a man standing by a campfire, cooking breakfast. At first, it seems like the normal response to grief that we often have when we lose someone we love. There are moments, walking down the sidewalk or stepping into a coffee shop, where we swear that we see that person we loved. Peter probably assumed that his eyes were playing tricks on him. But as he got a little bit closer, it became clear: Jesus was alive.

When they had finished breakfast, Jesus said to Simon Peter, "Simon, son of John, do you love me more than these?" He said to him, "Yes, Lord; you know that I love you." He said to him, "Feed my lambs." He said to him a second time, "Simon, son of John, do you love me?" He said to him, "Yes, Lord; you know that I love you." He said to him, "Tend my sheep." He said to him the third time,

"Simon, son of John, do you love me?" Peter was grieved because he said to him the third time, "Do you love me?" and he said to him, "Lord, you know everything; you know that I love you." Jesus said to him, "Feed my sheep. Truly, truly, I say to you, when you were young, you used to dress yourself and walk wherever you wanted, but when you are old, you will stretch out your hands, and another will dress you and carry you where you do not want to go." (This he said to show by what kind of death he was to glorify God.) And after saying this he said to him, "Follow me." (John 21:15–19)

Peter got scared. Peter got bold. Peter got brave and joyful and worried and over-thought almost everything. Peter took risks and Peter got hurt and Peter found himself once again invited in by the Savior he had denied just three days before.

An actual risk involves some feelings. It involves a little healthy anxiety and some sadness and some excitement and maybe a little bit of confusion. Taking risks looks a whole lot like being a human. My friend Livi and I were talking about this idea that Peter is such a fickle person and how it's insane but also encouraging that he is so loved by Jesus. Livi remarked, "Peter is a demonstration of the fact that there's no 'best guy for the job' where Jesus is concerned. He just wants people—messy, scared, brave, beautiful people."

When it comes to risk or safety or bravery or fear or any situation we may face, my encouragement to you is this: He knows you're scared, but He knows what is on the other side. Like a parent who is ready to catch a small child jumping into the swimming pool, He not only asks you to jump, but extends His arms to catch you. Every risk is met with the arms of a loving Father. Every leap of faith is toward a good and kind God. Every bold step into the unknown is moving us along, closer to Jesus. Feel your feelings, even if that means stepping into the dark trembling, but by all means, take a step forward, knowing that He knows what's on the other side.

She's not going to stay dead. The child will be the Savior. His touch will bring peace. It's not a ghost. The body hasn't been stolen.

It's not what you think.
It's not what you think.
It's not what you think.
Do not be afraid.

CHAPTER NINE

Kingdom Instinct

I t was my last year of seminary, and the word that comes to mind when I think of how I felt is "panicked." I wasn't entirely sure what I would do after school, but I knew that I wanted to be calculated about it. One of the parts of growing up people don't often put on Instagram is the pressure you feel before whatever's next. You see the photos of goofing off during study sessions or posts about how ready someone is to be done with school, but underneath that surface layer exists another layer of fear and uncertainty. Every well-meaning person who asks you what your game plan is going to be after graduation might as well twist the knife of "I don't know but I'll pretend that isn't bothering me" deeper into your back.

Sometimes, when we're in a particularly fragile place, we get really concerned with being safe. It's a natural tendency in all of us, but we have to be careful to still listen to the voice of God, even in days of distress. I wish I could tell you I did just that. I wish I could say I trusted Him, but I didn't. Instead, I did that thing where you try to grasp at plans and control and I started applying for jobs that would keep me safe.

Specifically, I started interviewing for a job doing communications administration for a church.

It wasn't really in my lane but I knew I could do the job, so I did what anyone would: I sat down with Jesus and explained to Him my plans. Five years at this job would be steady work in a decent town and I could pay off student loans and have job security. Then, after the five years, I'd consider what it was that Jesus had put into my heart three years earlier.

It wasn't that I didn't want to pursue the calling I'd sensed God put in me; it just wasn't the kind of calling that paid well or provided benefits or put me in a place of comfort. I applied and got interviews and they went well, and I ignored the screeching monkey on my back that was losing its proverbial mind every time I inched closer to locking in the job offer.

February came and with it a gathering of women in Boston I was helping orchestrate. I was there taking photos and keeping my distance from the messages being preached about risk and trusting God when suddenly a dam broke in my heart during a time of prayer. I walked up to a woman that I didn't even know, and I confessed through tears, "I am afraid that if I trust God with my future, He's going to send me to some dangerous mission field and I'll die and I know that He probably wouldn't do that, but I have to confess that I don't trust Him with any of my future. At all. And I don't know what to do—or if anything can even be done about it—but I can't live like this anymore."

I went home with an overwhelming fear that Jesus was going to ruin my life. It's hard to describe that kind of grieving surrender, but I want to try to explain it, because I'm certain I'm not the only one. It's a sadness over letting go of control. You know it's for the best, but still you cling to the idea that you are relinquishing control. You grieve the loss of safety and certainty and clarity. Of course, none of this was ever in your hands to begin with, so you're really just coming to grips with reality.

I got a call for a final interview and an offer at the safe job. I walked in, and after a few minutes, I finally followed some kind of gut instinct and said, "You know, my heart beats for women in the Church knowing Jesus, and it just really doesn't break for any of what this job is." I explained to the interviewer my lack of trust in God, and he looked at me and said, "Oh, yes, I see. You clearly need to pursue that instead."

I walked out with a skip in my step like when Anne Hathaway throws her phone in the fountain in the movie *The Devil Wears Prada*. I told my friends I had turned down the safe job and would be jumping instead into the unknown. I felt like a dang hero.

When you take a great risk and turn down security in pursuit of something else, you have that feeling of when you're jumping into a cold pool and you're right above the water thinking, *Oh, dear. What have I done?* People will look from the outside and cheer you on, reminding you that you are the dang hero you believe yourself to be because people like a good story. They love a risk (as long as it's not their own), and they will tell you that you're doing the brave thing, knowing full well that they wouldn't trade places with you for a moment.

What I wanted in that moment of risk was to feel immediate payoff, but sometimes life returns to normal disappointingly fast. Eventually, the excitement died down. The application for graduation was filed, and more and more people were dying to know what I was going to do next. I sat down and wrote a dozen or so e-mails to women who were working in the field I wanted to get into, and it felt like embarking on an adventure.

Some of us grew up in a generation that was told that adventure and hype were the only way to do your faith. If something wasn't upside down or on fire for Jesus, you weren't working hard enough. You weren't really living out the gospel if it wasn't some spectacular experience day after day. This has made us unrealistic at worst and cynical at best when we realize that the real work of the Kingdom can't be sustained this way. Man does not live on hype alone. Not one bit. You could be a stay-at-home parent, a small business owner, a CEO, or unemployed, and still take risks. Sometimes, that risk looks like leaving a job or getting really honest with your kids or asking for forgiveness. What matters most is a willingness to walk into whatever it is that Jesus has for us, even when that seems a bit scary.

Part of what contributes to this obsession with *epic* is the fact that social media is giving us an unrealistic expectation of what normal life even looks like. We scroll through Facebook or Instagram on our phones in moments of boredom, looking for another thing to occupy our minds and what we're met with is the carefully filtered and edited versions of people's lives. There we sit, in the middle of *meh*, as we scroll through beauty and joy and relationship. It's no wonder statistics prove higher levels of depression in people who spend more time on social media. Still, part of us keeps scrolling, and as we start to feel inadequate, we assume the best answer is that we just need a more exciting life. This is where the pursuit of epic falls short.

What you don't see on social media are the arguments and slamming doors and crying alone in the bathroom. You don't see the letters of rejection or job termination, or hearing the doctor explaining it's not likely that children can be had naturally. You're not in the spaces that haunt the lives of those people in your feed who are smiling at you. You're not actually seeing the real world, but instead are seeing a projection of the life we wish we always had.

Take one look at my Instagram, and you'll see dinner with friends, FaceTime with my nieces, or beautiful mountain ranges. But honestly? I eat a lot of the same kind of sandwich every day and make dinner alone a good amount of the time. You won't see photos of the cold I had last week or the pile of bills I have to pay.

Still, the craving we have to do something epic and amazing leaves us feeling like failures. But when you measure success by Instagram likes and Facebook reactions, you'll never be satisfied.

If the only actions that count are public moments of excitement and achievement, you'll go to bed exhausted and empty-handed. Sometimes, the act of offering your company or a text of encouragement or a letter in the mail is the greatest way to follow a holy, Kingdom instinct that God has put in our very souls. It is not epic, but it is everything.

Daily obedience always makes up the character we're trying to fabricate in other places. There's no shortcut to cultivating that kind of appearance. Our actions, great and small, speak for themselves.

As I ventured into the unknown of turning down safety based on my Kingdom instinct, I waded into the murky waters of *What have I done?* I started to accept that I was a fool, and with every day that no one was answering my e-mails, I considered running back to the safe job. Everything in me wanted to go back to security at any cost.

In the Book of Joshua, we meet a man who is about to take the helm of leadership, and his hands had to have been shaking. The previous leader of the Hebrew people was a man named Moses, arguably the best leader of all time. He had led them out of slavery, through the Red Sea as the waters split, and they followed a pillar of fire and smoke in their journey. And that was just the first few months of his tenure. At the end of his life, Moses went to the top of a mountain alone and looked out over the Promised Land, and as the sun set, he found himself face to face with his Creator. The Lord took him, and the people he had led wandered around in mourning over the loss of a great man, and as they dried their tears, they looked to Joshua to lead them to the land they'd been waiting for generations to inherit. I think the phrase we're looking for here is "a tough act to follow."

The Lord calls to Joshua and starts the conversation with, "Moses my servant is dead" (Joshua 1:2). Talk about a real motivational speech. He's reminding Joshua this isn't the time to compare yourself or look to the past. Rather, an era has ended, and it's time to push forward. It's time to take the people of God farther than they've ever gone before, and whether he likes it or not, Joshua is the man for the job.

Joshua isn't rushing into this, eager to outdo his predecessor. Over and over again, God tells Joshua to be strong and courageous. That's not something you say to someone who is confident and sure. It's something you say to someone who has one eye on the door.

The Bible is full of trembling leaders and anxious messengers and uncertain warriors and skeptical trailblazers. And while some of them got to do some pretty incredible stuff, none of them got there without being obedient in small ways and seemingly insignificant moments.

Joshua stood and listened to what the Lord had planned. Travel and battles and lots of fear stood in the way of the Hebrews and their Promised Land. But over and over again, God promised Joshua that He would advocate and fight for and lead the people. His words were meant to comfort and guide the fresh, nervous leader. With the words of the Lord still ringing in his ears, Joshua commanded the army to start the trek forward.

For years, I've been an avid golfer, and during seminary, I worked on an old New England course and occasionally would fill in as a caddy, spotting the trajectory of players' golf balls and learning to keep a sharp eye on exactly where they landed. One afternoon after class, I took my golf clubs and went to the hillside near my house. It was going to be dusk soon, but I found a small joy in hitting golf balls back and forth across the yard. I would stand about 100 yards from a big tree and knock a golf ball over its branches into the patch of dark grass on the other side. As the sun started to sink, I found myself having to use my caddying skills of seeing the ball contrasted against the dark sky. Finally, I hit one a bit too late, and it was lost into darkness. I ran over to search it out but came up empty. I went back to where I'd hit it and reimagined it landing and bouncing and followed the trajectory to where it should have been. But found nothing.

Evening was descending and the temperature was dropping but something desperate in me ignited, determined to find that little white ball. I abandoned my other golf clubs and walked every inch of the grass, breath turning to vapor in front of me, nose turning red with chill. Someone might argue that it was a waste of time to do such a thing. But something down in me knew that the golf ball had to be there. I had seen it.

I had seen it.

I prayed for a miracle and paced back and forth, shoes taking on the cool dew of evening.

The Kingdom of God is a simple nudge sort of instinct that almost, at times, feels like a fleeting thought. You see a person who is homeless, and you pause to consider helping them out. Your child asks for one more story, and you decide to oblige. A friend pops into your mind one afternoon so you send them a quick text to offer a word of encouragement.

I wonder if perhaps we have lost the art of Kingdom instinct. We make excuses or avoid the extra effort, and the person on the corner doesn't even look up and the child goes to bed and the friend continues with life as usual without the notification of your text message. It doesn't seem to be something that creates a big change in our day, and we assume it won't make one for them, either. But sometimes, in moments of desperation, we need another person to bring us to a place of hope or wonder or awe. We need someone to remind us we exist in a Kingdom that is eternal and unshakable and at our fingertips.

The notion of the Kingdom isn't realized one day, long from now. It's the narrative of a good King and his good Kingdom and the people who fill it. It's for yesterday, today, and forever. (See Hebrews 13:8.) It stretches to eternity and meets us here and now, and when we follow the instinct to bring it back into focus, the world is made better and made new in some small way.

I had no job prospects and the timeline for finishing school was coming to an end. I called my college mentor, Shelly, and told her everything—how I thought I was being brave but now I felt foolish and like I'd given up a future that was certain and replaced it with nothing substantial. I told her I felt lost and unprepared and she reminded me of Joshua. And there, like standing in the dark looking for a golf ball in tall grass, I caught a glimmer of the hope of the Kingdom of God in the form of a friend believing on my behalf when all felt lost.

If the beauty of the Kingdom surrounds us, and we are called to proclaim it, the enemy wants to silence us. He wants you and me to believe that the person who is homeless or the child or the friend doesn't need to see the Kingdom. He makes us second-guess and doubt that simple Kingdom instinct in the hopes we will retrain our eyes to see less. If the Kingdom gives us eyes to see, the enemy will do everything he can to distort the image.

Satan isn't very passive. He doesn't tell lies occasionally. Scripture reminds us he's actually the father of lies (John 8:44)—juxtaposed against Jesus being the way, the *truth*, and the life (John 14:6). And we know the devil is like a prowling lion, seeking to devour us (1 Peter 5:8). Last time I checked, devouring wasn't a casual sort of thing. No, devouring ruins and maims and murders. I'm not saying always look over your shoulder, but I am saying don't be shocked when you find yourself believing lies.

To follow the simple instinct of the Kingdom is to tell the truth. To show things as they really are. To cut to the point and speak words of life and honesty. To be straightforward in our desire to care for each other. To follow the simple instinct of the Kingdom is to step up and say, "I'm in."

Jess and I met our first year of college. She's the kind of friend that you just hold dear all the time. One night, a few months into freshman year, she walked into our friend Jamie's room and I don't think she was expecting me there. She'd come to talk about something that needed prayer, but instead of shying away since someone else was in the room, she welcomed me into the conversation. I was amazed by her honesty and understanding of what community really means, and it's one of the fondest memories I have of her.

A few months later, I came home on spring break for a friend's wedding. It was a beautiful ceremony and reception on one of those perfect North Hollywood afternoons. Afterward, I hitched a ride back to my parents' house with some of the wedding party. What had been a pretty ideal day suddenly shifted when I walked in the door.

Something heartbreaking had happened, and I was met with a tremendous grief. Unsure of how to respond, I opened my phone and called Jess. I told her what was going on, and she didn't hesitate before simply saying, "Melis. Say the word and I'll come to you."

There she was, with her family on spring break, several plane rides away, and it was very clear to her that what she needed to offer was her presence in a tough moment, even though it would cost time and money. I'm sure she had plans and needed rest, but she still sat there, simply offering herself to me. It could have been awkward to throw out such a crazy idea, but instead it steadied me.

This is what I mean when I say the Kingdom of God is simple: It's a gut instinct that we learn to listen to over time. It's a nudge or a whisper that reminds us that this time that we hoard and the schedules we protect and the to-do lists we manage are actually not the main thing at all. It isn't an over-planned list; it's the kind of thing you sense and push into.

Things settled down and Jess stayed in Colorado, where her parents lived, but her offer continued to haunt me and challenge me to think in different terms. I still cry almost every time I tell the story, because even though it was a simple act, that simple act is significant. In a moment of intense fear and grief, God healed me through the words she spoke. He healed me with the understanding that I was not alone. And it felt rare, because these Kingdom instincts seem to get lost most of the time.

After Shelly reminded me of Joshua's shaky start, she offered one other thought: This Kingdom instinct? The nudge to follow the Lord? It isn't going away anytime soon. We don't get to check "risk career for something else that Jesus may have planned" off the list and move on. No, to seek the Kingdom means to surrender our plans and our control continually.

In Joshua 13, much has happened in the life of our now-weathered leader. He has crossed into the Promised Land and seen entire cities collapse and the people of Israel set stones as a memorial for all that the Lord has done. He saw the sun stand still and led conquests across the land. One would say that he had accomplished his to-do list. Instead, the Lord says to Joshua, "You are old and advanced in years, and there remains yet very much land to possess" (Joshua 13:1).

Can you imagine? I'm sure the last thing that Joshua wanted to do was keep going. I mean, God led with, "You are old and advanced in years." It's mentioned in Hebrew twice for emphasis. He's old—like really, really old.

Still, Joshua presses onward. He continues to listen to the Lord because he knows that the Lord's way is always the best way. When we see Jesus reveal His Kingdom in small and big ways over time, it causes our hearts to align a little closer to His, and as a result, we find confidence in His ways because they are *always* better than our ways.

Had I followed my own instincts and taken the safe job, I wouldn't have sent the e-mails to people I admired. I wouldn't have gotten a response weeks later from a woman who wanted to get coffee. I wouldn't have met her and the women she worked with. I wouldn't have applied to work at that ministry. And on the last day of finals week, I wouldn't have gotten a phone call, offering me a job that turned into one of the greatest blessings of my life.

That job gave me lifelong friends and a deeper love for writing and Jesus and risk-taking. It actually got me to where I am writing this book right now, at a retreat surrounded by women who ache to see the Kingdom of God. And with every answered e-mail and new friendship and experience, my faith in who God is becomes stronger. He came through in that season of risk and doubt in ways I never could have imagined, and now when faced with the opportunity to take a risk, I know who is on the other side, and I willingly say, "I'm in."

Joshua was told to be strong and courageous so many times because God was preparing him to lead. And by the time he was old, I wonder if he shook his head and a smile broke across his aged face when the Lord said, "Let's keep going."

A few chapters later, in Joshua 23, he gathers together his leaders and says to them, "You have seen all that the LORD your God has done to all these nations for your sake, for it is the LORD your God who has fought for you" (v. 3). He knows full well that God is the one who carried them to where they are.

The night was cold and dark, but finally I spotted the round white surface of that golf ball. I could hardly see anything else, but as I bent over and picked it up, I threw my fist to the air in victory for no one to see. No one else was there to witness what felt like a small miracle but with a swing in my step, I walked back up the hill to my house, full of faith that wasn't there before.

As we see what God has done, it gives us confidence

He'll keep showing up. He has never failed to be present. His Kingdom has never failed to exist. If we only have the instinct to seek and the eyes to see—even in the dark—that there is simple goodness to be found, proclaimed, and embraced.

CHAPTER TEN

Where Do We Go from Here?

I remember the January before I finished seminary because it was one of the clearest images of the gospel that I have ever known. The golf course was open only until Thanksgiving or so when the snow of New England would force it to be closed until April, or whenever everything melted. Therefore, I was on a pretty tight budget. My saving grace was that my room and board at school had already been paid for by a scholarship I was on.

And then, one afternoon, I found out that there was no meal plan during the one-month-long January term. I honestly didn't know how I was going to be able to afford any food and started to panic. That, paired with the whole "give up the safe job opportunity" cliff jump I'd just done, meant that nothing felt stable. I had no idea where I'd end up vocationally after school finished in just a few months. I had no way of paying for groceries, but I had a heart full to the brim with pride, so I pretended everything was okay, even though I was overwhelmed in every way.

On the following Sunday, I was walking the hallways of my church when my friend Laura saw me. She asked me how I was, and I basically burst into tears over it all. "I just don't know what I was thinking," I said, panicked. "I mean, I don't remember a moment when I felt like seminary was what I was supposed to be doing. I just applied and came here and what if God doesn't have a plan for this and I'm not supposed to go into ministry? How can I help other people if I don't even have anything to give?"

She waited for me to finish my emotional rant and finally said to me, "Melissa, I will believe on your behalf that you're supposed to be here. That you're supposed to be in seminary and God knows what He is doing. I will believe it for you because you can't believe it right now for yourself." That afternoon, there was a text from Laura that her husband, Clayton, was at my house. I went downstairs and was greeted by an out-of-breath friend who had carried a box through the snow from the parking lot down the hill.

Red-nosed and smiling, Clayton said, "It's not much, but I brought you this."

In the box was a loaf of bread and a gallon of milk and supplies for sandwiches and some Kix cereal.

"We had extra because we always need these things with kids at home. It should help you get through some of the month." He handed me the box and explained there was a bit more food in his car, so he walked away to get the second load. I carried it up to my room and sat there, overcome by how tangibly Laura and Clayton had loved me. I looked at the cans and loaves and jam and peanut butter and I wrote this down:

Sometimes, you wonder how you're going to feed the poor and help those in need when you have no income. And someone sees you and hears you and loves you. And they feed you because for a moment you are one in need. And you come undone a little bit over how years later He still provides loaves like He did for five thousand. And it's smaller, but no less miraculous.

Every act of community is a small miracle because so much of us is tempted to disengage. To sit this one out and not show up and refuse to let ourselves ask for help. We're always trying to prove our own ability to do all the things by over-extending and overcommitting while at the same time never asking for the support we need when we need it most. Our pride and our desire to be put together do us in every single time. But as we've unpacked in the last nine chapters, there's a give-and-take involved. We have to be honest enough to ask for help—or at least admit our imperfections—and we have to be free enough to give and show up for each other.

> Every act of community is a small miracle because so much of us is tempted to disengage.

The Kingdom and Presence of God is a call-and-response. It involves leaning in and pulling back and knowing when to speak and when to be silent. It's a relationship with our

Creator that sets us free to be in relationship with one another in a way that is good and kind and has the right motives. If we show up only because we want to look good, we've missed the point because we've made it about us, not about Jesus. If we only share the beautiful part of our lives and neglect to look underneath the rug, we are putting up a fake front and no one can truly know us in the ways that God wants us to be known.

But when we are willing to be seen and see each other? Something powerful starts to happen, and we are able to catch a vision of how God's Presence is our good and His Kingdom is our aim. When we see one another as co-heirs and fellow pilgrims, we stop objectifying and start loving well. I wasn't Laura and Clayton's project—I was their friend and fellow sister in Christ. And they weren't my saviors; they were my friends and vessels through which God showed me His love.

> When we see one another as co-heirs and fellow pilgrims, we stop objectifying and start loving well.

What happens when we live into the Kingdom and Presence of God? We pause our lives to show up in someone else's. Jesus doesn't just want us to know that He's safe and good and in control and that our work has purpose and we can take risks just for the sake of us knowing. No,

He wants us to put that knowledge to use and to build His Kingdom.

We are told that the Kingdom of God—that is, the realities that we can experience now—is given to those who follow God. Matthew 18:4 says, "Whoever then humbles himself as this child, he is the greatest in the kingdom of heaven" (NASB). It's not for those who make much of themselves or work to protect their own interests.

In Luke 6:20, we are told, "Blessed are the poor, for theirs is the Kingdom of heaven." Again, humility and setting ourselves aside are the keys to understanding the Kingdom. Pretty much everything that refers to the Kingdom has an upside-down-ness, though, right? The last become first and the first become last. The children are wise and the prideful fall. The way of the cross is even one of sacrifice—a King who not only walked among His people, but became like them and suffered humiliation. The sooner that we wrap our minds and hearts around this upside-down way of living, the sooner we can get down to the hope of the Kingdom: that all is made new again.

We are under a King who is not only good and kind but also active among us. He is binding up the brokenhearted and calling us to do justice and love mercy. (See Micah 6:8.) He is a God who has entrusted us with the gospel not so that this legacy of faith will sit on a shelf, but so that we will get up and actually do something with it. That we will not hoard it or study it or ponder it only, but give it away freely. Faith without works is dead. Theology without action ceases to be good theology.

So let's go back to the start and walk out what these chapters look like put into action. First, if the Kingdom and the Presence of God are real, we have to repent. This means we have to get really honest about where we're at and stop, turn around, and try it God's way. His way, the way of the Kingdom, is our truest north. And when we walk away from it, we're venturing into dangerous territory.

Sometimes that means we have to confess to one another, and it always means we have to confess to God. When parts of our lives live in darkness, they grow darker and harder to carry. Christ calls us to bring things out into the light and speak truth over one another. We know from His character and promises that He is gracious and slow to anger and abounding in steadfast love. While it can be uncomfortable to get really honest about the state of our souls, we are promised that He makes us as white as snow. He takes our sin and our shame, and He redeems every last inch, but we have to get real about our need of Him.

Practically, then, we have to find a few fellow believers who will get real with us. We have to find a community of people who not just love us well, but confront us well. There's a difference between someone who just says, "Well, it's okay. God still loves you," and someone who says, "You are still loved, but something is going on here that needs to be addressed." True friends will get really straightforward (and you can do that in a loving way!) when it comes to destructive patterns and behaviors. Find those people who make you share what's actually going on and push you toward the cross. Be so bold as to say, "I need someone to walk this out with me and pray over this." Don't know where to begin? Ask someone who is a bit further along in their faith journey to come alongside you.

I recently spoke with a woman who has spent years with a college ministry, and when I asked her about this, she said, "You know, the way people say it nowadays is that they want a mentor. But by definition, a mentor is teaching you how to do a thing. It's more like an apprentice. What we need is someone to disciple us. A disciple-maker is someone who will teach you how to be in an actual relationship with Jesus." This is what we are after, friends: actual discipleship. Not someone to just listen to you process and send you on your way. No, we need someone who will actually love us enough to show us Jesus and speak the truth to our situations until we learn the rhythms of relationship with Him for ourselves. We love because Christ first loved us (see 1 John 4:19), which means that we are called to live out what we have been given by giving it to other people. No excuses, no conditions. This is not what we *have* to do; it's what we all *get to do.*

If we are living in the reality of God's Presence, we will have confidence in who He is and that will change everything about how we view ourselves and the world around us. In fact, who we are and what we bring to the table are very much related to who He is. As people made in

197

His image, we are carrying that around with us all the time. That means when we love and when we speak and when we encourage and when we challenge, we are doing it as someone who is made in the image of the One who invented all of those things. He is a real, living, loving, speaking, encouraging, challenging Creator who longs to be with those whom He has created.

Lived out, this looks a whole lot like checking our egos and our words and our presuppositions at the door. It means we care about people's relationships more than their résumés. We use our words to bring life and truth (even when that's hard) rather than tearing others down or manipulating them. We must be measured in our anger and abundantly wild with our love. We are not here to prove ourselves, for we have been given the gift of the gospel, which tells us that He is enough for all of us and we will never lack. I don't care if you lost your job or your hope or your identity or your home—you are found in Christ and He is abundant. He does not stop, He does not lack, He is our everything and our more than we could ask or imagine (see Ephesians 3:20).

And as if it isn't enough that He has done and is doing great and beautiful things in the world around us and with His nearness in our daily lives, we are promised that He will extend these things into eternity and that hope allows us to continue to do the good work He has prepared for us. Long before you picked up this book or heard the name of Jesus, He knew what gifts you would have and what heartache you would endure and He is eager to walk out every single mile with you as you walk out every mile with the community that He has given you.

Because God is safe and trustworthy, we can hand Him our fears with certainty that His aim is to redeem us. Over and over again, He is the God of redemption. Naomi and Ruth and Peter and Moses could all tell you right now that they had lost all hope but God blew their minds with His grace and goodness and ability to save them from any situation. Every person in Scripture that is revered for their faith was beyond rock bottom at some point but our trustworthy God lifted them out because that's what He does. It doesn't mean life will be nothing but easygoing, rich prosperity—sometimes the opposite happens—but it does mean that we can rest assured that He is doing work in our hearts and communities that we don't even see.

Jenn and I were talking about a story that seemed really hopeless last week, and I remarked, "I don't see how it'll work and there's nothing in the works [to redeem the situation]." Without missing a beat, she replied, "Something is in the works, we just aren't privy to it yet." And y'all— I didn't get it. I wanted to be, like, "No, really. Nothing is in the works." But then I realized what she was saying. Before we're even born, there's a plan. Before we speak, He is speaking. Before we move, He is moving.

Before I sat here in Nashville, before I lived in Austin and Boston and Chicago. Before my childhood and before my parents decided to get married while unloading the dishwasher. Before all of it, He set things into motion. It is always, always in the works.

And so when we face the unknown—the singleness or the moving truck or the new job or the diagnosis—it's never not in the works. Hear this, friends: Things might feel stuck and hopeless and broken today, but one day? One day we will sit around and laugh, and someone across the table will sigh and quietly reflect, "Huh—I guess it was in the works that whole time." If that doesn't preach, I really don't know what does. May we see clearly what is not always clear and rejoice in the freedom of not knowing everything. Take heart: Something is in the works.

The beauty is that we are told in Scripture how it all ends up. We are promised in Revelation 22:20 that Jesus is coming back. And when He does? All the brokenness of the kingdom of man that is touched by sin will be restored. Revelation 21:3–4 says:

And I heard a loud voice from the throne, saying, "Behold, the tabernacle of God is among men, and He will dwell among them, and they shall be His people, and God Himself will be among them, and He will wipe away every tear from their eyes; and there will no longer be any death; there will no longer be any mourning, or crying, or pain; for the first things have passed away." (NASB)

That whole thing where God wants to have communion with us and will move everything around so we will feel our way toward Him? This is the end result. This is the goal He has in mind that will come to pass. He will dwell with us and among us, just like in the garden at the start of the story. He will wipe away our tears, and there will no longer be sorrow or death because Christ has conquered death. All these things pass away.

This is perhaps why I so adore that creation narrative and the last chapters of Revelation—because it's all full circle. We are told that Adam and Eve sinned and death entered the world, but here, we see that Christ's power conquers the grave, and when He comes, we will know that victory in completion. No more death. No more pain. Nothing but the work of Jesus Christ making all things new as the old ways (which we are currently having to wrestle with) come to an end.

If we go back even to the very start, as the Spirit of God was hovering tremendously, anticipating the words "Let there be light" in Genesis 1:3, we see that the end is also light.

The account in Revelation continues:

> *And the city has no need of the sun or of the moon to shine on it, for the glory of God has illumined it, and its lamp is the Lamb. The nations will walk by its light, and the kings of the earth will bring their glory into it. In the day-time (for there will be no night there) its gates will never be closed; and they will bring the glory and the honor of the nations into it. (21:23–26 NASB)*

The cycle of Kingdoms and Kings that was there in creation is now seen in its fullness—a light so bright that there's no need for any reinforcements. And just as Christ doesn't give us salvation but *is* our salvation, He doesn't just give us light—He *is* the light. The Presence and Kingdom will consume us completely. Everything will be the way it was intended.

So what does this mean for us now? It means that we have a lot of Good News on our hands. It means that the Kingdom isn't just here, but it's there, too—in its fullest sense. And if we know what's coming, we can walk in confidence that this life we're part of right now is only the beginning of a very long story of God's beauty and grace. And we can see how God's Presence and His Kingdom are meant to be part of every day leading to their fullness. That means that when we talk to our neighbors and our children and our siblings and our co-workers, we get to do so with joy and with hope and an unshakable assurance that our work here and now is not wasted. None of it is wasted.

Every conversation and every action and every moment that we are living out our faith is an opportunity for Jesus to be known. I used to think that evangelism looked a lot like asking people if they were ready to trust their whole lives to a God they really didn't know. And I was taught growing up that the main point of heaven is to get out of hell. And while those two things are true, they aren't the motivation for what we do at all.

When we are motivated by fear and guilt, we're not entering into a real relationship. And telling people about Jesus by framing the gospel through only a lens of what happens after we die is like being a coffin salesperson. Who cares what happens after we die if we won't even be there? Why would anyone trust a God who they don't know? What use is a Kingdom that we can't see and a Presence that we don't feel a lot of the time?

These questions are legitimate, but they're missing the main point: Jesus isn't just for eternity—He's also for this moment. He's also for today. He's also for whatever you're facing. You are not alone and you are seen and you are known and you are loved deeply by God, who aches to be with you. And because you were made in His image, you have inherent worth and value, and the work you do every single day does not define you anymore. In a world that measures you on performance and social status, this is, simply put, good news.

When a person goes to the doctor, Jesus is sitting there in that extra chair they keep in the corner. When someone is stuck in traffic, He's the passenger beside them. When a bride is walking down the aisle and the groom won't stop crying at her beauty, He's whispering, "This is only a reflection of how much I love you." He is there when you spill your coffee and get a promotion and hear news of your grandmother's death. Every moment is saturated by the Presence of God, and when we recognize that, we can't help sharing these truths with the people around us. We can't help telling our friends who don't know Jesus that they are seen and loved and known. We can't help carrying one another's burdens because He carried ours first.

We become a pay-it-forward people when we encounter the Good News.

Here's the thing that I am learning as I sit here on my kitchen floor, wrapping this whole book up: The Kingdom and Presence of God are everywhere and they change everything. When we are secure in that? We can face what was once hard with freedom because we have the long view. When we rightly know who God is, we stop creating Him in our own image and walk in the newness of life. When we learn the rhythms of His nearness, we let ourselves have some grace for a change. When we see our work as God-ordained and good, we stop treating clients like burdens and our co-workers like competition.

And the best part of how these realities change everything is this: We get to tell this story to everyone. In the way that we pray and cheer and weep, we are telling the story that started so long ago and continues into forever. We get to take our place in the Kingdom and proclaim, "I once was lost but now am found, was blind and feeling my way toward Him and now I can see." We can stop trying to stake our claim by being the most educated or interesting or clever and recognize that we inherit everything and so do our brothers and sisters in Christ. No one is better than anyone else. Everyone has a seat at the table. My pastor preached this: When the Kingdom is here, it will be a party.

The story started in darkness and ends in light. The people of God can't stop changing, but God Himself stays the same. We are looking forward to perfection and restoration, but today? We have work to do. We have a Kingdom to help build and proclaim and give out to those who are lost. We have a Presence to soak in and learn from and take comfort in. He gives us good things and He carries us through hard things, and even when all seems lost, we can remember that He knows the way and He loves us tremendously.

ACKNOWLEDGMENTS

This book was a miracle I never saw coming, and I doubted that it would really happen for over two years of my life. I was told growing up that I'd be a writer by teachers and friends, but I never dreamed it'd happen like this. So, let's start at the start.

Thank you to my family. My mother offered me her legacy of creativity and my father came to the United States in pursuit of the American dream and now we are here raising the next generation. Thank you, Mom and Dad, for not freaking out too much when I said I wanted to be a writer and for giving me a camera when I was a kid so that I could learn to tell stories. Thank you to my siblings and siblings-in-law for loving me and being patient with me in this process. Laura, Thomas, Maddy, and Rick, you are one heck of a home team. Thanks to Emma, Constance, Myra, Bonnie, Georgia, and baby on the way for being the best nieces I could hope for. You remind me to still look

around in wonder. Steve, Taunji, and CJ: Y'all are my family and I'm who I am because of you.

Hannah and Sarah came to Nashville to help me outline
this book over a long weekend. Their input helped me put
this mess into motion and I am forever indebted to them
for this. And thanks to Bethany and Stephanie for cheering
me on so very early in this process.

I was raised by strong women who modeled to me that
the local church is a good, good thing. Thank you to Leslie,
Debbie, Barb, Susie, Jeanette, De, Taunji, Alice, Hannah,
Mary, Sue, and Rosie. This crew has been there since birth
and watched me grow up into the Kingdom of God.

Anna and Chris: You show me how to live loved.

College friends, specifically the girls of Ten West and
the iNfoRmaL team: You brought these stories to life.
Thanks for growing up with me.

Seminary friends; thanks for walking with me through
all kinds of seasons and not taking this book too, too
seriously. We're all still a bunch of kids trying to learn
Hebrew on very little sleep. Kristin, Joelinda, Britt, Kyle,
Katy, Burton, Anne, Andrew, Charis, and countless others:
Thank you for seeing me through it all.

IF girls: Thanks for watching me fall apart both literally
and figuratively. Jennie, Lindsey, Brooke, Jordyn, Amy,
Lisa, Aly, Elizabeth, Delkies, J-Pay, Bre, Hannah, and
Sam—that year was a good year, even with the mice in the
office. Karen, you watched me cry a lot and you were really
nice about it and taught me to be authentic.

I sat in counseling chairs the last ten years and it dramatically changed how I saw Jesus. I owe a debt of grati-tude to Steve Brasel, Patricia Vander Sande, Rachel Hilker, Dana Doerksen, Cynthia Fisher, and Alicia Lewis (she's the one who says most of the wise things in this book!). I also want to thank Rachel Schuelke, who was my very first counselor back when I was a college student. I was young and just beginning adulthood and she changed my life.

MinnConnTenneCo: You girls have prayed me through it with patience and kindness I'll never be able to repay. Brenda, Allison, and Rachel: You keep me honest.

To my teachers over the years who loved me and told me I could write: Patti Duncan-Rice, Rex West, Mr. Muff, Lindsey Hayes, Jamie Janosz, Sharon Beynon, Karyn Hecht, Pam MacRae, Dr. Gwenfair Adams, Dr. Jim Singleton, and so many others.

Thank you to those who read early drafts and prayed over every inch of this. Specifically, Amanda May, Margaret Rose Jones, Jess Hites, Amanda Privett, Cassandra Johnson, David and Anna Westfall, Chesney and Preston Hill, Adam and Jennifer Jones, Jessica Pederson, Will Cottrell, Polly and Adam Woods, Will Boyce, Miranda Roberts, Alex and Annie Kato, Matt Blazer, Dan and Jan Gudim, Nathaniel and Audrey Adkins, Lauren Baber as well as Julie Lenocker and Tiffany Ong.

Here's to the Nashville crew that kept me afloat. Andrew and Jamie Peterson, your hospitality allowed this book to be written in a place that reminded me of the beauty of the Kingdom and Presence of God. Father Danny, Sandra McCracken, Kelsey Miller, Nina Coyle,

Mindy Cook, Janelle Hiroshige, Jordan Grassi, Ivanna Lenk, and Mary-Michael McCathren. Also, Margaret and Brady and the team at Results Physiotherapy: You helped me rebuild when I kept wrecking my back by sitting and typing for days on end.

Berean Bible Fellowship: You raised me. Holy Trinity Church Chicago: You encouraged me. North Shore Community Baptist church: You are my home. Sarah, Joe, Laura, Clay, Beth, Stephen, Natalie, Lianna, and so many others: Thank you for cheering me on. Bobby and Julie: You lead with love and the honesty I need. Tim and Ann: You are my New England parents and I love you so deeply. To the ladies of St. Mary's who carried me with their love: Melinda, Susan, Debbie, Poppy, Ann, Beth, and Flo.

Hey, Camp Well girls: You're gamechangers. Jenn, Kelly, Cheryl, Cassie, Kelsea, Andee, Emily, Taylor, Jackie, Amy, Maria, Christi, Sara, and Sarah: You're gonna change the world.

To those who were good friends when I needed it most: Savannah Conner, Seth and Amber Haines, Heather Korpi, Ashley Lampkins, Ana Wrede, Clare Richardson, Shelly Stevens, Kelly Stuckey, Lindsey Wheeler, Rebekah Lyons, JJ Heller, Ellie Holcomb, Amanda Williams (who believed in this book before I had a clue what was coming and even bought me Sharpies to start brainstorming), Vivian Mabuni, Angie Smith, Meredith Toering, Jo Saxton, Angela Sammer, Mindy Blagg, and Christina Hankins (and all the girls at the Tuesday night Bible study, to which I am late because I'm writing this). Jackie, thanks for buying me Chick-fil-A so I could make this happen and still get dinner. The Beasley family and Jensen family who have housed me as I worked through edits—you are the best. Taylor Leonhardt: Your words made all the difference. I love being a young creative with you. Sharon Miller: You gave me confidence when I was about to lose it. Annie Downs: You treated me like an author, and it was a gift and a half. East Nashville neighbors: thanks for not thinking I was crazy when you saw the crazy outline for this book on my kitchen wall.

Austin and Kendall and the team at Wolgemuth: you will never know what having a stellar literary agency has meant. You are making dreams happen and I'm honored you chose to sign me before anyone else.

To Virginia and the team at FaithWords: Thank you for partnering with me and trusting me to write these words down. You took a tremendous risk and I'll forever be grateful that you made me an offer.

You people need to know that Grace P. Cho was a massive force behind this book. She stayed up late editing and processing and carrying these words into the world. She is the *Eemo*, or auntie, of this book, and I'll never express how her patience, wisdom, and incredible way with words allowed this book to exist.

To my co-workers at Masterworks who put up with me being pulled in two directions for a whole year. To my PNW friends: Heather B., Heather R., Sara, Alex, Josh, Tara, and Paige.

I am certain I forgot someone here. But man, what a blessing to get to be so very loved.

Jesus, I don't know how to thank You for this book or these people. And it feels so very small to express, but I have to whisper it over and over again: *Thank You, thank You, thank You.* You really are good and faithful and strong for reasons that have nothing to do with this book, but I see those things in this whole journey.

Melissa Zaldivar holds a master's degree in theology from Gordon-Conwell Theological Seminary. As a freelance writer, she has told the story of Jesus in contexts from Bible studies to articles with a voice that is young and honest. Walking through intense experiences throughout her life, she has learned that God is constantly present, even during the darkest of seasons, and desires to share that perspective with her readers. She blogs at MelissaZaldivar.com, where she wrestles with the intersection of theology and the ordinary. She lives in Nashville, Tennessee.